A Handbook for Young Writers

Jonas Lane

First edition. 31st March 2024

Copyright © 2024 JONAS LANE.

Written by JONAS LANE.
Published by Jonas Lane Publishing

Good Luck!
Jonas Lane

First published 2024.
©2024 Jonas Lane.

Publisher's Note:
This is a work of non-fiction inspired by great teachers, educators and writers from all around the world.

The moral rights of Jonas Lane to be identified as the author of this work has been asserted by him in accordance with the Copyrights, Designs and Patents Act, 1988.

All rights reserved. No part of this publication may be reproduced, stored in a retrieval system, or transmitted in any form or by any means, electronic, mechanical, photocopying, recording or otherwise, without the prior written permission of the author and publisher.

Published in Great Britain.

Cover Design by James, GoOnWrite.com

A Handbook for Young Writers

Jonas Lane

First edition. 31st March 2024

Copyright © 2024 JONAS LANE.

Written by JONAS LANE.
Published by Jonas Lane Publishing

Contents

Foreword...page 7

Young Writer's Vocabulary...page 3

Young Writer's Spellings...page 136

Young Writer's Checklists...page 150

Index...page 172

A Handbook for Young Writers

About the author

Jonas Lane is an acclaimed author and educator who is never happier than when he's telling a tall tale, whether it's to his readers or the children he teaches daily. He has written several books across a number of different genres, including the hugely popular Lord Thyme-Slipp series, regularly fusing historical fact with hysterical fiction

Although predominantly classified as a children's and YA author, Jonas Lane's books appeal to all ages, his reading audience being those that are still young at heart. Every novel Jonas has had published so far has been rated as 5-star by those who have reviewed them, young and old

In addition to writing novels, Jonas Lane is also a published poet and has written articles both locally and nationally, as well as being a former television and music critic for the Bedfordshire Times.
Jonas lives in North Bedfordshire with his wife and cats….

Visit Jonas at his website
www.jonaslaneauthor.com

Foreword

I have only recently realised that I retrained to be a teacher almost twenty years ago. In that time, I've lost count of the resources I've read, researched, written, created or adapted to help my children both in school and the writing clubs I've run to help develop young writers. Not only that, but the time spent printing or creating smart boards and PowerPoints, laminating and binding word mats, as well as putting up displays to help them must run into weeks, if not months, possibly years....

It was only after realising this and much, much more that I decided to compile everything once and for all into a handy help book that all of my young writers in years 3 to 6 could refer to and borrow, use, adapt or improve on any examples given in their English lessons, in and out of school, to aid and develop their own vocabulary skills and independent writing.

I make no apology for not going into full and complete grammatical detail on everything they are taught or expected to know in Key Stage 2 as – frankly – it would turn them off writing forever were I to remind them of every single facet of the English language which is drilled into them daily. Hence the fact that this is a writer's *handbook* to help support and enhance their writing rather than being a dry and dreary grammar book which would send them to sleep instead by being far too technical and complicated!

A Handbook for Young Writers is aimed at being a quick, user-friendly guide to help *my* writers with their ideas, vocabulary, creativity, and flow by providing them with a broad range of useful and helpful information, as well as providing lots of examples they can borrow, use, improve upon or adapt for themselves, along with reminders as to the spelling rules they are also expected to know and remember.

There is some deliberate repetition in this handbook as words belong to so many different words classes and be used for many different reasons (no wonder our primary children and young writers get so totally confused). These over-complex grammar rules inhibit my young writers rather than help them to write freely. By repeating them occasionally, children will hopefully find what they are looking for under the heading they've been told to refer to or when searching through the book and its index.

Ultimately though, as I myself am a writer first and foremost, this book has been put together to do what I want it to do – support my children in and out of the classroom setting with their English writing skills as well as helping to free their creativity so that they develop a lifetime love of writing for pleasure and purpose...

Will *A Handbook for Young Writers* replace the need for the quality first teaching of grammar and English? – *no*.
Will it be the only book my children will ever need to refer to again when they are writing – *definitely not*.
Will my children be able to use it immediately to help improve their writing skills and knowledge – *absolutely!*
I hope that it also does the same for your young writers should you have chosen to give them this book as I've done with all the children I work with on a daily basis.

Jonas Lane

JONAS LANE'S HELPFUL HINTS ON VOCABULARY

'This sentence has five words. Here are five more words. Five-word sentences are fine. But several together become monotonous. Listen to what is happening. The writing is getting boring. The sound of it drones. It's like a stuck record. The ear demands some variety.

Now listen. I vary the sentence length, and I create music. Music. The writing sings. It has a pleasant rhythm, a lilt, a harmony. I use short sentences. And I use sentences of medium length. And sometimes when I am certain the reader is rested, I will engage him with a sentence of considerable length, a sentence that burns with energy and builds with all the impetus of a crescendo, the roll of the drums, the crash of the cymbals—sounds that say listen to this, it is important.

So, write with a combination of short, medium, and long sentences. Create a sound that pleases the reader's ear. Don't just write words. Write music.'

Gary Provost

ADJECTIVES

Adjectives are words used to describe and give more information about a **noun**, which could be a **person, place** or an **object**...

Examples of adjectives you could use to describe feelings: angry annoyed anxious ashamed bewildered cheerful confused courageous defiant depressed determined disgusted disturbed eager elated embarrassed enthusiastic envious excited fantastic frightened hungry lethargic lonely

Examples of adjectives you could use to describe people: adorable aggressive annoying beautiful caring confident considerate excitable glamourous grumpy important intimidating mysterious obnoxious talented weird

Examples of adjectives you could use to describe size and shape: big colossal enormous gigantic great huge immense large little long mammoth massive mighty miniscule minute obese petite puny short tiny

Examples of adjectives you could use to describe time: ancient brief early fast late modern old quick rapid short slow swift young

Examples of other adjectives you could use in your writing: beastly brotherly burly cowardly dastardly deadly deathly elderly ghastly ghostly giggly gravelly grisly heavenly holy kindly leisurely lively melancholy miserly monthly northerly otherworldly prickly quarterly rascally saintly scaly shapely sickly slovenly southerly spindly sprightly squirrelly stately steely surly swirly timely ungainly unlikely unruly wily wrinkly

ADVERBS ENDING -LY

*An **adverb** is simply a word that describes a verb (**action or doing** words like **run, fly, read, be** etc.). e.g. He **quickly** ate his breakfast. Below are examples of adverbs which end with -ly.*

(SEE ALSO ADVERBS NOT ENDING -LY AND ADVERBIALS)

A - abnormally abruptly absently absentmindedly absolutely accidentally accusingly actually adventurously adversely affectionately always angrily annually anxiously arrogantly awkwardly

B - badly bashfully beautifully bitterly bleakly blissfully boastfully boldly bravely breathlessly briefly brightly briskly broadly busily

C - calmly carefully carelessly cautiously certainly cheaply cheerfully cleanly clearly cleverly closely clumsily colourfully commonly compassionately confidently constantly continually continuously conveniently coolly correctly courageously crisply cruelly curiously

D - daily daintily dangerously darkly dearly deeply defiantly deliberately delicately delightfully desperately determinedly diligently dimly disgustingly distinctly doggedly doubtfully dramatically dreamily

E - eagerly easily effectively elegantly energetically enormously enthusiastically entirely enviously equally especially essentially evenly eventually evidently exactly excitedly exclusively expertly extremely

F - fairly faithfully famously fatally fearlessly ferociously fervently fiercely finally fondly foolishly fortunately frankly frantically freely frenetically furiously

G - generally generously gently gleefully gradually gratefully greatly greedily grumpily guiltily

H - harshly hatefully heartily heavily helpfully helplessly highly hopefully hopelessly hungrily

I - immediately impulsively inadvertently increasingly incredibly initially innocently inquisitively instantly intensely intently interestingly inwardly irritably

J - jealously jestingly jokingly jovially joyfully joyously jubilantly judgmentally justly

K - keenly kindheartedly kindly knowingly knowledgeably kookily

L - lawfully lazily lightly likely limply lively loftily longingly loosely loudly lovingly loyally

M - madly majestically marvelously meaningfully mechanically meekly mentally messily mindfully miserably mockingly mostly mournfully mysteriously

N - naturally nearly neatly negatively nervously normally notably

O - obediently obnoxiously obviously occasionally oddly offensively officially openly optimistically originally outwardly overconfidently

P - painfully partially patiently perfectly playfully pleasantly politely poorly positively possibly potentially powerfully predictably professionally promptly proudly

Q - quaintly quarrelsomely queasily queerly questionably questioningly quickly quietly quirkily quizzically

R - rapidly rapturously rarely ravenously readily really reassuringly recklessly regretfully regularly reluctantly repeatedly righteously rightfully rigidly roughly rudely

S - safely scarcely sedately selfishly separately seriously sharply sheepishly silently simply sleepily slowly slyly softly speedily steadily sternly strictly stubbornly successfully suddenly suspiciously sympathetically

T - tenderly tentatively terribly thankfully thoroughly thoughtfully tightly totally tragically tremendously triumphantly truly truthfully typically

U - ultimately unaccountably unbearably undeniably understandably unexpectedly unfairly unwittingly

V - vaguely vainly valiantly valuably variously vehemently vengefully venomously verbally vertically viciously victoriously vigorously vilely violently virtually visibly vitally vividly vocally volcanically voluntarily

W - warily warmly wastefully weakly wealthily wearily weekly weirdly wheezily wholeheartedly wickedly widely wildly willfully willingly wisely wishfully wistfully woefully wondrously wordlessly worriedly worryingly wretchedly wrongfully wrongly wryly

X, Y & Z – xenophobically xerographically yawningly yearly yearningly yieldingly youthfully zanily zealously zestfully zigzaggedly zonally

ADVERBS NOT ENDING -LY

*Although the majority of **adverbs** end with -ly to give us extra information about **how, when, where,** or **why** something is happening, here are some examples of adverbs which don't...*

(SEE ALSO ADVERBS ENDING -LY AND ADVERBIALS)

A - about above abroad across after afterwards again ahead alike all almost alone along aloud altogether always anywhere apart around ashore aside

B - back backwards before beforehand behind below besides beyond

D - dead deep doubtless down downstairs downwards

E - either else elsewhere enough even ever everywhere

F - far fast forever forth forward furthermore

H - half hard here high home how however

I - in indeed inland inside instead

J - just

L - late less like likewise little long loud

M - maybe meanwhile moreover much

N - near neither never nevertheless no nonetheless not now nowadays nowhere

O - o'clock off often on once only opposite otherwise out outside over overall overhead overnight overseas

P - parallel past perhaps please

Q - quite

R - regardless right round

S - seldom short since so somehow sometime sometimes somewhat somewhere soon still straight sure

T - that then there thereafter therefore this though through thus tight together tomorrow tonight too twice

U - under underground underneath up upright upwards

W - when whenever where wherever wide within worldwide

Y - yet

ADVERBIALS

*Adverbials are words or phrases which have been used like an **adverb** to add detail or further information to a verb. They are also used to explain **how, where** or when **something** happens. Adverbials can be used in different places in a sentence. If a **preposition** is used instead, they are then called **prepositional phrases.***
(SEE ALSO FRONTED ADVERBIALS AND PREPOSITIONAL PHRASES).

Examples of adverbials of occurrence – explaining *how often* something happens: continually... generally... often... usually... occasionally... periodically... seldomly...
always... all the time... hardly ever...very often/seldom...
every now and then/now and again/so often etc.
every minute/day/week/year etc...
once in a while/blue moon/lifetime etc.

Examples of adverbials of manner – explaining *how* something happens: crazily... as quick as a flash... gracefully... cautiously... with hope in your heart... stupidly... gently... easily...as soon as possible... with fear in her eyes... viciously...as swift as the wind... without warning...

Examples of adverbials of possibility – explaining *how likely* something will happen: almost certainly... definitely... maybe... surely... possibly... obviously... perhaps... probably... undoubtedly...quite likely... impossibly... improbably... unquestionably...

Examples of adverbials of place – explaining *where* something happens: on the ground/bench/roof etc....
beside the window/bed/door/tree etc....
somewhere far away/out there/far from here etc....
all around the world/the Earth/the planet/the globe etc.
over by the fence/the river/the bush/the bridge etc.

out in the open/the fields/the meadow etc.
between the cliffs/the gates/the pillars/the mountains etc.
down in the valley/the gutter/the basement etc.
beyond the clouds/the stars/the gates etc.
along the road/the country path/the street/the way etc.
back at home/school/grandma's/my friend's house etc.

Examples of adverbials of time — explaining *when* something happens:
straight away... later on... sometime later... soon...
earlier that day/afternoon/evening/night etc.
all of a sudden... before the end of the day/night etc.
in the morning/afternoon/evening etc.
as soon as possible... without delay...
next week/month/year etc.

ADVERBS - COMPARATIVE AND SUPERLATIVE

*A **comparative adverb** is used to compare two actions whilst a **superlative adverb** is used to compare three or more. When an **adverb** ends with -ly, you must use **more** to form the **comparative adverb** and **most** to form the **superlative** one.*

Adverb	Comparative	Superlative
effectively	more effectively	most effectively
frequently	more frequently	most frequently
recently	more recently	most recently
seriously	more seriously	most seriously
slowly	more slowly	most slowly

Examples

*Could you play your music **more** quietly please?*
*Jonas Lane spoke **more** slowly to help the children understand the question.*
*The **most** frequently I'm asked question is how do I get my ideas.*

However, if a short adverb does not end with *–ly*, then the **comparative and superlative adverb** is then identical to **adjectives**. e.g. You add the suffix **-er** to form the comparative adverb and the suffix **-est** to form the superlative. Also, if the adverb ends in **-e**, remove the letter before adding the suffix.

Adverb	Comparative	Superlative
fast	faster	fastest
hard	harder	hardest
high	higher	highest
late	later	latest
long	longer	longest
slow	slower	slowest

Examples
*Humphry works **harder** than Gilbert does.*
*100 m sprinters all run incredibly fast but Usain Bolt was the **fastest** sprinter of all time.*
*It was the **longest** night of his young life.*

WARNING!

However, some adverbs don't follow these rules and have ***irregular comparative and superlative*** forms just to confuse you yet again....

Adverb	Comparative	Superlative
badly	worse	worst
far	farther/further	farthest/furthest
little	less	least
well	better	best

Examples
*H.G. Wells' time machine travelled **farther** than Lord Slipp's Time Skipper ever could.*
*Manchester United are playing **worse** than they did last week.*
*Lionel Messi is easily the **best** player ever.*
*Turning lead into gold was the **least** of Poppy Copperthwaite's worries.*

ALLITERATION

*Alliteration happens when words which start with the **same sound** (not just the **same letter**) are used repeatedly in a **phrase** or **sentence** for added effect. They are great for tongue-twisters too...*

Examples of alliteration

A ferocious fairground of faltering fear.
A murderous mansion of mischievous mayhem.
A pitiful pool of putrefying pain.
An oval office of outrageous and open honesty.
Cheeky Charlie Chalk is a Czech chess champion.
Cunning Carlos Cuthbert collects colourful Columbian clothes.
Eager Eddie Edwards edits excellent e-books every evening in Edinburgh.
Hopefully, Humphry hauled his heavy hammock high over his head.
Marvin Martin's malevolent motorway of miserable mischief moved menacingly.
Naughty Nigel Neal's nephew needed a new notebook.
Perfect Poppy's piglet playfully pranced pathetically.
Silly Slipp sleepily staggered down the slippery stairs.
The shimmering star of sympathetic sorrow.
The wailing waterfall of whispering wonders.
Trudy's tormented temple of tremendous terror.

ANTONYMS

Antonyms are words which have the opposite meaning to another word. e.g. **antonym** is the opposite to a **synonym**! You can also create an **antonym** sometimes by simply adding a **prefix** to the **root word**, making the new word the opposite to the original word...
(SEE ALSO PREFIXES)

Examples of antonyms

agree - *disagree*
cold – *hot*
correct - *incorrect*
destroy - *create*
divide - *unite*
finished - *unfinished*
good - *evil*
happy - *sad*
huge - *tiny, minuscule, minute*
increase - *decrease, reduce, shrink*
lazy - *energetic, hyperactive, lively*
love - *hate, detest, despise*
near - *far*
quiet - *noisy*
real - *fake, phony, bogus*
sunrise - *dusk, sunset, twilight*
tall - *short*
understand - *misunderstand*
young - *old, mature, adult*

APOSTROPHES FOR CONTRACTION

*The definition of the word **contraction** means **becoming smaller**. Therefore, when writing you can use an **apostrophe** to combine certain words together to make it shorter with the **apostrophe** replacing **the missing letter(s)**. **Contractions** are especially useful when writing informally.*

*Here is a list of the most common **contractions** for you to include in your writing - checking that you've put the apostrophes in exactly the right place of course!*

are not = *aren't*
can not = *can't*
could have = *could've*
could not = *couldn't*
did not = *didn't*
do not = *don't*
does not = *doesn't*
had not = *hadn't*
has not = *hasn't*
have not = *haven't*
he is = *he's*
he would = *he'd*
I am = *I'm*
I have = *I've*
I will = *I'll*
it is = *it's*
let us = *let's*
must not = *mustn't*

shall not = *shan't*
she is = *she's*
should have = *should've*
they will = *they'll*
should not = *shouldn't*
that is = *that's*
they are = *they're*
was not = *wasn't*
we are = *we're*
what is = *what's*
who will = *who'll*
will not = *won't*
would have = *would've*
would not = *wouldn't*
you are = *you're*
you have = *you've*
you will = *you'll*
you had = *you'd*

APOSTROPHES FOR POSSESSION

*Apostrophes are also used to show **possession** – **who** or **what** something belongs to, adding the apostrophe to the end of their name.*

Poppy Copperthwaite's spellchecker.
Lord Slipp's time travelling machine.
Humphry the Boggart's lunch box.
Miss Fletcher's temper.
Watson's bed.
Cordelia Wilde's apartment.
Miss Morgan's blade.
The dragon's scales.

APOSTROPHES FOR PLURAL POSSESSION

*To show **possession** when the **noun** is **plural** – when there is more than one someone or something - and already ends with the letter **s**, you add the apostrophe to the end of the **plural** word instead.*

The Dragon Chasers' weapons.
The twins' robes.
The werewolves' footprints.
The racing drivers' cars.
The dragons' den.

Take care though as adding an ***apostrophe*** to words which are already ***plural*** like ***men***, ***women*** or ***children*** can be tricky as they don't end with the ***letters s***. With these, you add an apostrophe to the end of the word, then the **letter *s*** to show possession.

Examples
The children's sorcery lessons.
The women's fighting clothes.
The men's battle armour.

CHARACTER DESCRIPTION

*One of the most important things a writer needs to do is provide the reader with information describing their character, especially if they want them to know exactly what they look like, remembering to use **show not tell** wherever possible of course...*

Examples of words you could use to describe a character's body: angular athletic big broad bulky burly chubby fat frail lanky lean lithe muscular narrow overweight pint-sized plump podgy scrawny short slender slight slim small stocky stout tall thin tubby underweight well-built wide willowy wiry

Examples of words you could use to describe a character's facial features: attractive bearded bespectacled birth-mark blotchy button-nose cheerful chubby clean-shaven dark-skinned dimples disfigured double-chin eye-patch egg-shaped fair fat five-o'clock shadow flushed freckled freckly goatee beard good-looking gorgeous handsome hideous hook-nosed kind lips long loving miserable misshapen mole morose moustache mutton-chopped narrow odd olive oval pale pale-skinned pasty plump pocked pointed pretty prominent rosy-cheeked round rounded scarred shadow sideburns spotty square-jawed squint striking stunning sullen sunburnt sunken-cheeked tanned thin-lipped ugly unshaven unsightly unusual warts wicked witch-like wrinkled wrinkly

Examples of words you could use to describe a character's hairstyle: afro bald balding bewigged bleached bob braided braids bun closely-cropped coarse combover cornrows crewcut crimped curly dark dreadlocks dyed fine floppy frizzy gelled ginger golden greasy greying highlighted luscious man-bun messy mohawk neat over permed pigtails plaited plaits ponytail rat-tailed quiffed ringlets shaved short-back-and-sides shiny skinhead spiked tangled thick thinning tramlines unkempt unruly wavy wild wiry wispy

Examples of words you could use to describe how a character might move: awkwardly blundering edging hobbling limping lumbering marching looming pacing plodding racing scrambling skulking shuffling stalking stooping striding strutting stumbling sweeping trudging waddling ungainly unsteadily

Examples of words you could use to describe how a character's voice sounds: booming breathless clear confident croaking echoing flat gravelly gruff heavily-accented hoarse hushed inaudible incoherent laboured loud nasally quiet quivering raspy rambling shrill weak wheezy whispering unintelligible

Examples of words you could use to describe how a character's dressed: classically-dressed dishevelled eccentrically-dressed expensively fashionably-dressed impeccably immaculately ill-fitting modern modestly old-fashioned plainly pristine scruffy shabbily-dressed shabby simply smartly-dressed spotlessly suited-and-booted stylishly tattily tidily tramp-like unkempt untidy vintage well-dressed well-groomed worn

CHARACTER / SETTING NAMES

Sometimes the hardest thing to do when writing a story is think of the names of the characters you'll meet or places you'll visit, especially when you're world-building. Here are some tips and tricks that you might like to try to help you pick exactly the right ones....

Search through lists or books of baby names – Often, all you have to do is go through a list of baby names either by looking through specialist books or by visiting online baby name sites. You could also ask your family what you might have been names other than the name you were given! e.g. I was due to be called *Laurie Light* who is now a character in *Nona's Ark!*

Create names out of everyday words – In the past, family names often reflected the trade of the head of the family, like *Butcher, Baker, Tanner* etc. so think about these types of profession names too, tweaking with the spellings a little as J.K. Rowling did with Kreacher the elf in Harry Potter.

e.g. *Lucy Teecher, Kali Barba* etc.

Alternatively, you could take an everyday object and make that into the name of one of your characters. e.g. *Ed Wood, Jenny Bell, Kristina Tongue, Ruby Willow* etc.

Mix up the names of people you know – Of course, you could just take the names of people you know and switch them around to create brand new ones...

e.g. John Hartson, Phil Mole and *Sheila Bridges* become *John Mole, Sheila Hartson and Phil Bridges!*

Make your names fun! – It's your story after all so you should get a kick out of the characters you're writing about. *Bottom, Worm, Gilbert Tootler, Worzel Gummidge* and *Mr Stink* are names which immediately put a smile on your face as soon as you say them and will remain known by readers long after their stories have been told.

Think of names from your own past – Often you'll come across a name of someone you meet that just sticks in your mind for some reason - both good and bad! These can sometimes provide you with the inspiration needed when creating a character. However, remember to not be deliberately cruel or unkind though, especially if your character is based on someone that you know quite well or that they know you...

Turn real people's names around to see if that works - Sometimes family names can be switched around with first names and then adapted to create a character.
e.g. Adam Mason became Mason Adams in Wilde and Dangerous Things

Add hyphens, prefixes or suffixes – Another good way of creating character names is by using different forms of punctuation, along with *prefixes* and *suffixes.*
One of the favourite pieces of punctuation I use is the *hyphen* as adding these between family or place names can make them even more memorable to your reader.
e.g. Lavinia Arbuthnott-Splott, Lord Augustus Thyme-Slipp, Alexander McClellan-Jones, Camestone-on-Ouse etc.

Then, to help make your character stand out even more and make them seem unique or important, you could always give them a title by using a special *prefix*.
Prefixes like *Sir, Lord* or *Mister* can help add some formality to your character, similarly, noble titles and *hyphened* names are also significant if you're writing about a different time period as it makes your writing seem more realistic and believable.
e.g. *Ms., Mrs., or Mr. Sir or Madame, Doctor, Colonel, Captain, Major, Constable, Lord or Lady, Duke or Duchess, Father etc.*

Just as *prefixes* can be added to the front of a name, *suffixes* can have exactly the same effect when added to the end of your

character's name.
e.g. *Henry the Eighth (VIII), Tom Jones Junior, Doctor Marcus Welby M.D.* etc.

Attempt alliteration – A great but simple way of creating a character or setting name is by using alliteration. This is especially true in comic books and graphic novels.

e.g. *Sue Storm, Reed Richards, Peter Parker, Clark Kent, Lois Lane, Prospect Place* etc. However, try to only include one or two characters/places named this way - unless you want everyone in your story to be alliterative of course!

Time to rhyme! – Another fun way to create a name is by making the first and last names of your character or setting rhyme. e.g. *Sue Magoo, Glenn Penn, Upper Supper, Chicken Licken, Foxy Loxy* etc. Again, try and use them sparingly though.

Use words from other languages that you know or are familiar with *(as long as they aren't too rude or course!)* – When George Lucas first wrote Star Wars, he tried to come up with an unusual word for an alien species which he eventually named the Calamari (which is Italian for squid) though Admiral Ackbar has always looked more like a giant shrimp to me!
JRR Tolkien wrote that Bilbo Baggins lived in Bag End which is directly translated from the French phrase *Cul De Sac.*
In *Dragon Chasers*, there are a race of people called *Sárkány* (which is Hungarian for dragon) who are led by a character names *Vezető* (which means leader in Hungarian too).

Names with a secret or hidden meaning - If your character(s) have an air of mystery or malevolence about them, or are vital to the plot in some other way, one popular method you could use is by giving them a name which has a secret, hidden or

double meaning. It could be a word which is a synonym for another or a foreign or technical word which links directly to the character's personality or role in the story.
  e.g. *Moroi, Cogheart's Madame Verdigris, Lily Hartman, Silverfish, Mould and Roach etc.*

Find words that are seldom used anymore — when world-building it is often easy to use words that are not commonly used in everyday language anymore, hence in *Slipp In Time*, Lord Thyme-Slipp (a play on words himself) lives in *Codswallop, Blinkingshire*. Other places in this fictional county of mine are *Scallywag Bay, Balderdash, Bunkum* and *Piffle,* all based on words now seldom heard or used in everyday life.

Create an anagram of a real name — Of course, you could always create a name by finding an anagram of an original name instead.
e.g. Jason Lane, Jon A Slane, Jona Slane, Jason Lean, Alan Jones, Jonas Lean, Jason Neal, Jonas Neal are all anagrams of *Jonas Lane,* whereas if you're looking for a unique or unusual location *Manchester* transforms into *Amerstench,, Amensretch Carmenseth Chanmerest* and *Smeartench!*
In *Poppy Copperthwaite, Gilbert Tootler* is a near anagram of my oldest and closest friend's full name. Can you work out what it is?

Look for names that are ancient, classic, no longer popular, are dying or have died out — Similar to using words not commonly used anymore, have a look at popular name lists of the past to identify names you could use. These are especially good when writing something not set in the present day.

  e.g. *Copperthwaite, Tristan, Ophelia, Garry, Alan, Henrietta, Light, Plantagenet, Lancaster, Tudor etc.*

Choose a name that fits the period you are writing about – It is also important that your name suits the time period you are writing about. This is quite easy to do if writing something set in the present day.

However, when writing about the past, make sure that you use names which were most popular then - names like *Anne, Mary, Elizabeth, James, Edward* and *William* are more accurate than the likes of *Dave, Chelsea, Cristiano, Tinkerbell, Snowflake* or *Buttercup*! Biblical names are also good ones to use as they have been around for a very long time indeed. e.g. *Matthew, Mark, Luke, John, Abigail, Esther, Ruth* etc.

Pick a name which matches your story setting – Equally important is to have a name which matches the nationality of your character, hence an American could be called *Hank Martin III* whilst someone from Africa might be named *Emmauel Maccabeus* or something similar.

If you can't find a name you like then make one up! – There's always the chance that you just can't come up with something that works or that you like. Therefore, create a new one entirely before checking if anyone else also has that name in real life. This was an approach I took when writing *Poppy* Copperthwaite, creating a whole host of character names especially suited to fit her magical universe.

e.g. *Oswald* and *Fenella Gogglewick, Norris Rongen* and *Leopold Harryhausen* to name but a few...

Take common, everyday words and change them slightly to suit your needs and purpose – In Peter Bunzl's brilliant Victorian adventure book *Cogheart,* he used the term *mechanimals* for animals which are clockwork powered whereas George R.R. Martin changed the honorific *Sir* to *Ser* when naming his knights in his *Fire and Ice* series of books.

It is also a technique I have used, having a magical race of people called the *Majeek* who all *Come of Mage* at the age of eighteen in my book *Poppy Copperthwaite*...

Abbreviate real names, merge them together or just add some punctuation — George Lucas' classic *Star Wars* is a perfect example of how to do this with *R2D2* being an abbreviation of the movie term *Reel 2 Dialogue 2* and *C3PO* being the *California 3 Post Office* near where he lived at the time.

Examples I've created in the past have included names I've combined together like *D'alan, T'alex, S'harry Tomoliver, Ethanella* and *Bella-Ann*.

Use real place names to help create characters or locations — Been somewhere with a memorable or unusual name? Then use it as a character.

Rufus Stone, Barry Island, Leighton Buzzard, and *Newton Abbott* are all places in England and Wales. As for settings, in the classic television series *Star Trek*, there was once an exotic blue planet called *Luton* in an episode after its creator, Gene Roddenberry once landed at the airport there, so anything goes!

Have names which are a play on words — I also have a lot of fun with names which are either puns or a *play-on-words*, some of which have a double-meaning or fit my character's personality well...

   e.g. *Lord Thyme-Slipp, Patty Cake, Max Power, Phil Speed, Ben Down, Teresa Green, Humphry the Boggart* etc.

Online Character Name Generators — Finally, if you have eventually exhausted all possible avenues and are still stuck looking for that all important name - then go online and use one of the many character/setting generators listed there to help you find exactly the right one to suit your story. Happy name hunting!

CHARACTER / PERSONALITY TRAITS

Character or *personality traits* tell us more about the qualities or personal attributes which make up someone's overall character, either **physically, emotionally, mentally**, or **morally**...

A – abhorrent adventurous aggressive ambitious annoying anxious artistic arrogant athletic

B – bashful belligerent bossy brave brutal

C - caring chatty cheerful chauvinistic clever conceited confident conniving considerate courageous coward cruel

D – dodgy daring dependable devious devilish dishonest disloyal disrespectful dour dramatic dreary

E - eager egotistic elegant empathetic encouraging enthusiastic energetic excitable

F - fearless fierce fidgety fiery flexible focused foolish forgetful friendly frugal funny

G - giving gloomy greedy grim grouchy grumpy

H - hard-working honest hopeless horrible humane humble humourous hyperactive

I - imaginative immature impatient impolite inspirational intelligent intolerant irresponsible

J – jaded jealous jovial juvenile

K – keen keen-minded keen-witted kind knowledgeable

L – languid lazy lively loathsome loving loyal

M - mardy mean-spirited menacing miserable murderous moody

O - obnoxious open-minded optimistic

P - patient persistent pessimistic polite posh prejudiced proud

Q – quaint quiet quirky

R – racist, relentless respectful robust rude ruthless

S - selfish sensitive sneaky social solemn spoiled sullen stubborn

T, U & V – talented thoughtless tricky trustworthy troubled, temperamental unfriendly vulgar

W, X, Y & Z – weak-willed world-weary xenophobic, young-at-heart youthful zealous

COLONS

*Colons (:) are used to introduce a list, to help provide an explanation or to emphasise a point or piece of information. A **colon** can also be used after a greeting in a formal business letter, to present a quotation or to connect a series of related points but remember - you **do not** need to write a **capital letter** after the **colon**...*

Examples of colon use:

Alex knew that only three counties in England began with the letter D: Derbyshire, Devon and Dorset.

Cornelia Wilde had two choices: run away or stand and fight.

Everybody knew who'd win the match: Wales.

'Life is like a box of chocolates: you never know what you're gonna get.'

Mr Browne's favourite precept in Wonder is a quote by Dr Wayne Dyer: "When given the choice between being right or being kind, choose kind."

Nona Lancaster had always wanted to visit three Spanish cities: Barcelona, Madrid and Seville.

Remember this: two can play that game.

She has several favorite genres of books: fantasy, comedy, thrillers and mystery.

The pizza Humphry ate that night had several different toppings: cheese, bacon, pepperoni, salami, red peppers and onions.

The writer Stephen King says this is what you should remember when writing: "Description begins in the writer's imagination but should finish in the reader's."

Tristan offered us all the following advice: "Stare a dragon in the eye rather than try to flee from them if you value your life."

CONJUNCTIONS

Conjunctions – or connectives as they're sometimes referred to - link two words, phrases or clauses together, as well as being used to compare and contrast things...

COORDINATING CONJUNCTIONS

The seven most common coordinating conjunctions used to join sentences together are - for, and, nor, but, or, yet, and so...

Examples
Humphry packed a suitcase **for** the journey.
Poppy loves cats **and** dogs.
Gilbert doesn't like cabbage, **nor** will he eat Brussel sprouts.
Alex wanted to stay **but** Georgie wanted to go home.
Do you want cheese **or** would you prefer ham?
Jude was popular with them **yet** she struggled to fit in.
Patty didn't have any flour **so** she couldn't bake the cakes.

SUBORDINATING CONJUNCTIONS

Subordinating conjunctions normally introduce a subordinate clause, the most popular of them being - if, since, as, when, although, while, after, before, until, because...

Examples
Oswald Gogglewick will rule **if** Poppy doesn't Come of Mage.
She's been like this **since** they found her.
They all turned in for the night **as** they had an early start.
Humphry always eats two breakfasts **when** he wakes up.
Rob went to face the Sárkány alone - **although** terrified.
Lord Slipp carried on working **while** the children slept.
Nell skipped home **after** selling all of her oranges.
It was a few seconds **before** CJ realised what had happened.
Wilde knew she couldn't wait **until** later to do it.
He slept with the light on **because** he was scared of the dark.

COMPARATIVE CONJUCTIONS

These conjunctions - as well as, also, both, equally, in the same way, likewise, similarly, too - are especially good when comparing one thing to another, showing that they are alike.

(SEE ALSO ADVERBIALS)

Examples of comparative conjunctions

*Jonas Lane enjoys reading **as well as** writing.*

*Nona Lancaster can play in both defence and attack in football which, funnily enough, are **also** her favourite positions when playing hockey.*

*Mason saw there were dozens of similar sized houses on **both** sides of Baker Street.*

*Everyone agreed that the two of them were **equally** difficult to work with.*

*Georgie loved her mobile phone **in the same way** that Alex loved to devour his food.*

*Lexi worked hard to read the ancient text before her whilst Jude did **likewise**.*

*Julliette was late to the meeting with Wilde as I **too** was **similarly** delayed by the events that morning.*

*Mason knew that it was a case of **too** little **too late** and that he'd have to win her trust all over again.*

CONTRASTIVE CONJUCTIONS

*As you'd expect, these conjunctions - **alternatively, although, but, differs from, however, in contrast, on the other hand, whereas, while, yet** - show where something is different or opposite to another...*
(SEE ALSO ADVERBIALS)

*To purchase one of Jonas Lane's books, visit his website or, **alternatively**, order it from Amazon...*

*Legend says that werewolves exist **although** I've never seen one myself.*

*Lord Slipp wanted to travel back to Roman Britain **but** Alex and Georgie preferred somewhere warmer, like Ancient Egypt or the Indus Valley.*

*Cordelia's opinion of danger **differs from** that of her two closest friends, Mason and Julliette.*

*We will solve this mystery once and for all, **however** long it takes us to do so.*

*But once more, **in contrast** with their previous experiences, Slipp, Alex and Georgie skipped back into the past on their next adventure.*

*Sherwood Holmes, **on the other hand,** preferred the quieter surroundings of Scallywag Bay to London.*

*Foodball matches are allowed to use different fruits to play with **whereas** football teams are only allowed to use an official FIFA approved ball...*

*Silently, Rob slipped out during the middle of the night **while** Danny and Howard slept soundly in their beds.*

*It was a great source of frustration to Nona that major football tournaments were always shown on television **yet** foodball competitions never were...*

DASHES

*Dashes - not to be confused with **hyphens** - can be used in dialogue or to show that the speaker has been interrupted. They can also be used to show repetition of a word or phrase for effect. Of course, they are used to show **parenthesis** too...*
(SEE ALSO PARENTHESIS)

Examples of dashes

"Help me, Wilde," Mason yelled. "I think it's going to get-."
My favourite rock band – Foo Fighters – are touring the UK again this summer.
No - there's no way that's true, Kat - no - it can't be...
Pizza is my favourite thing to eat - after cheese, of course!
We're going to go back and put things right again - or at least we hope to...
Dragon Chasers: The Knight School is one of the greatest - if not the greatest - books of all time!
You should never argue with Miss Morgan - she can become quite angry and you wouldn't want to see that, trust me!

DETERMINERS

*Determiners are words that comes before a **noun** to introduce it and provide additional information about the quantity and proximity of the **noun** that's being written about. e.g. **this plate, some apples, several people** etc. They are then grouped as follows....*

Articles – a, an, the
Demonstratives – the, this, that, these, those
Possessives – her, his, its ***(note – an apostrophe is not needed here!)*** my, our, their, whose, your,
Ordinals – first, second, ninetieth, hundredth, next, last etc.
Numerical – One, Five, Ten etc., Hundreds, Millions etc.
Quantifiers – all, a lot, a lot of, any, both, enough, every, few, half, less, little, many, much, none, several, some, etc.

ELLIPSIS ...

*An **ellipsis** (**ellipses** plural) looks like three **full stops** written in a row (...) Most children think they are only used for cliffhangers. However, they can also be used to show longer pauses in sentences. **Ellipses** can be very effective in your writing but don't use too many as it can reduce their impact and make your writing harder to read...*

Here's how ellipses can be used effectively...
- To help you build mystery, tension and suspense
- To show hesitation in speech
- To help suggest that a character or the speaker wants to avoid saying certain words or thinks better of it
- To show that there have been words or phrases deliberately left out of the text quoted by the writer
- They can be used when writing a cliffhanger ending!

Examples using ellipses
They left about an hour ago ... I think ... or perhaps earlier ...
"Oh," said Auntie Flora, staring at Georgie's outfit, "that's ... nice, dear."
"I just wanted to say ... that ... I... will... always ... love... you..."
her voice crackled as she slowly faded away
I'm Poppy .... Phaedra Copperthwaite's my mother.
Tristan was uncertain whether to wake the dragon or not...

As mentioned, writers also use ellipses in direct quotes to show words or sentences which have been deliberately left out to make the quotation shorter and more concise. For example, look at this famous quote by the legendary child actress Shirley Temple:

"I stopped believing in Santa Claus when my mother took me to see him in a department store, and he asked for my autograph."

With an ellipsis it becomes: **"I stopped believing in Santa Claus when ... he asked for my autograph."**

EMOTIVE LANGUAGE

Emotive language is the way a writer deliberately shows greater feelings and emotions in their characters. Below are examples of words you could use in your writing to help put their emotions across more clearly...

Examples of words you could use to show feelings of happiness: cheerful contented delighted ecstatic eager elated enchanted energetic enthusiastic excited exhilarated gleeful high-spirited jubilant joyful keen light-hearted lively merry overjoyed pleasant pleased satisfied thrilled on top-of-the-world unruffled

Examples of words you could use to show that you/they care: adoring affectionate appreciative attentive compassionate considerate devoted doting fond friendly generous kind-hearted loving passionate respectful sympathetic tender thoughtful tolerant trusting understanding warm-hearted worshipful

Examples of words you could use to show anger: aggravated annoyed bitter enraged exasperated frustrated furious ill-tempered impatient infuriated irritated offended outraged resentful spiteful sullen tense ticked-off upset vengeful vexed vindictive

Examples of words you could use to show fear: afraid alarmed anxious apprehensive cautious defensive disturbed distressed edgy fearful fidgety frantic fretful frightened horrified intimidated nervous panicky petrified stressed terror-stricken threatened troubled uneasy unsettled watchful worried

Examples of words you could use to show confusion: baffled bewildered confused disorientated distracted dizzy flabbergasted flustered mistaken misunderstood mixed-up perplexed puzzled speechless startled stunned taken-aback troubled uncertain uncomfortable undecided unsettled vague

Examples of words you could use to show sadness: bleak crestfallen dejected depressed desolate desperate despondent dismal distraught distressed downhearted emotional empty fed-up gloomy glum grey hollow hopeless ill-fated low-spirited muted miserable sorrowful subdued tearful upset woeful

Examples of words you could use to show feelings of guilt: apologetic ashamed bashful disgraced embarrassed flustered foolish guilty hesitant humble humiliated mortified regretful remorseful repentant shamed shamefaced sheepish sorry wicked

Examples of words you could use to show feelings of hurt: abused annoyed belittled bereft crippled criticised crushed damaged destroyed devalued devastated humiliated imperfect miffed mistreated neglected put-down rejected resentful uncherished used wounded

Examples of words you could use to show feelings of loneliness: abandoned alienated alone blue cut-off dejected deserted despondent detached distant empty excluded forsaken isolated left-out lonely neglected rejected shunned withdrawn

Examples of words you could use to show feelings of weakness: broken defeated feeble flawed helpless incapable incomplete ineffective inferior insignificant lame overwhelmed powerless puny small uncertain unimportant unsure useless washed-up worthless

EXCELLENT ENDINGS

I'm often asked how I come up with the endings to my stories. To be honest with you, there's no right or wrong way - you just need to make sure it remains consistent with the tale you've told.

However, it's equally important to ensure your reader does not feel frustrated, disappointed or confused by how your story ends. Below are a few different suggestions - with some examples of course!

A surprising twist-in-the tale... - There's nothing more satisfying than getting to the end of a story expecting one conclusion, only to be left open-mouthed by a completely unexpected twist you didn't see coming...

Slipp stopped abruptly and stared back at the detective in utter disbelief.
"Uncle Jack...?"

Ending with a *'happy ever after'* - Nothing gives a reader a fuzzier glow than a happy ending, as long as you don't end with *"they all lived happily ever after..."* or my own, personal pet-hate ending *"they woke up and realised it was all a dream..."* Happy endings are great, especially if the characters have had traumatic or unhappy experiences but all works out in the end...

The old man smiled and placed his hand on Auggie's shoulder.
"Yes it is, my dear boy. Now, I want to pick your brains about how to time travel..."

Tissue reaching endings - By contrast, sad or unhappy endings can be more interesting and have a greater emotional impact, as long as they are subtle and not mawkish or overdone...

But it was the final three lines, obviously etched at a much later time judging by the font used, that would both warn and haunt Courtney to her dying day...

Linking the end of your story right back to its very beginning - Another way to end your story is to have it return to the beginning, possibly repeating some of the action your characters have already been involved in...

Back towards the lone house on the hill...
Back into history...
Back in time and on to their next adventure...

An open or unfinished ending - I like these as a writer because they always leave the reader wanting - or hoping - for more. With these types of endings, you can easily conclude one story whilst leaving the door open to the possibility of another, even if you have no plans for a sequel...

"That, cariads," I replied, kissing Megan and Aled gently on the tops of their heads before ushering them off the sofa towards the arms of their loving mother, "is a long story, best saved for telling on another, rainy day..."

Leave them wanting more with the hint of another mystery to come - Often, I feel a real sense of loss coming towards the end of a book I've particularly enjoyed reading. That's why I've always liked those where as one adventure ends, there's always the hint or a clue of another one just about to begin...

"Mr Adams...Miss Lumière...hurry," Wilde shouted, "go grab your belongings...we have a new hunt and it is already afoot!"

Make 'em laugh - You don't necessarily have to have a pun or a killer punchline at the end of your story - though they can be really effective if written well. Instead, if your tale has a character who was originally included as some form of comic relief, they could then deliver a final line or closing speech to leave a satisfied smile on your reader's face.

However, remember to ensure that it's in keeping with the character's nature and directly relates to the story itself.

"Soon everyone, Majeek, NORM and boggart included," Humphry declared, "will know the name of the greatest spellcaster the world has ever seen - Plopsy Smeltmybutt!"

And finally - everyone's favourite ending - the cliffhanger! - We all love it when the story ends with our hero's fate left hanging in the balance.
However, we need to ensure that any cliffhanger we write will genuinely make the reader want to know the final outcome of those they've spent so much time with when reading your story and have genuinely come to care about.
Nothing winds me up more as a reader when someone ends their story with "*What will happen next?*"
I don't know – you're the writer, you tell me!

What was that? That sound...like a gunshot...
And now I hear heavy footsteps slowly approach from beyond my chamber door...
James...?
Stoja...?
Anyone...?
Help me...

FRONTED ADVERBIALS

*Fronted adverbials are different **word classes** or **phrases** used at the start of sentences to describe the actions which follow, not forgetting a **capital letter** at the start of the sentence, with a **comma** after the fronted adverbial of course!*

(SEE ALSO ADVERBIALS AND PREPOSITIONAL PHRASES).

Examples of words you could use to show occurrence...

Again, Constantly, Every day, Every single second, Fortnightly, Frequently, Infrequently, Never again, Never before, Never in their life, Occasionally, Often, On rare occasions, Once in a while, Once or twice, More often than not, Rarely, Regularly, Repeatedly, Sometimes, Twice a week

Examples of words you could use to show manner...

Anxiously, As fast as possible, As quick as q flash... Awkwardly, Bitterly, Bravely, Carefully, Courageously, Curiously, Cunningly Defiantly, Frantically, Happily, Mysteriously, Nervously, Rapidly, Sadly, Silently, Slowly, Suddenly, Unexpectedly, Unfortunately, Wickedly, Without a sound, Without hesitation, Without warning

Examples of words you could use to show place...

Above the clouds, Around the back of the bike sheds, Back at the police station, Behind the curtain, Below the sea, Between the sea and the sky, Beyond the sea, Down by the river, Everywhere they looked, Far away from them, Here, In the distance, In the shadows, Nearby, North of here, Outside, Over my fence, Over there, Somewhere near there, There, Under the ground, Upstairs, Wherever they went,

Examples of words you could use to show possibility ...

Absolutely baffled, Almost unbelievably, Barely able to breathe, Completely exhausted, Decidedly shaken, Definitely confused, Hardly having broken sweat, Having just arrived, Maybe,

Much admired, Nearly asleep, Obviously angry, Pleasantly amused, Positively trembling with... Quite understandably, Somewhat flustered, Somewhat surprised, Totally overwhelmed, Utterly amazed

Examples of words you could use that show time...
After a second or two, After a short while, Afterwards, All of a sudden, Already, Always, As soon as I could, Before too long, Eventually, Immediately, In August, In the blink of an eye, In the evening, In the meantime, Just then, Last month, Later, Momentarily, Next year, On Saturday, Soon, Today, Tomorrow, Yesterday,

HOMOPHONES AND NEAR-HOMOPHONES

*Homophones are two or more words which are said the same way but have different spellings or meanings. (Words that are spelt the same way but which have different meanings are called **homographs**, e.g. **read** – 'read this book' and **read** - 'I've read that book!')*

accept *(to receive)* — except *(not include)*
add *(addition)* — ad *(advertisement)*
advice *(to offer suggestions)* — advise *(to recommend)*
affect *(to act on)* — effect *(result of an action).*
air *(oxygen)* — heir *(successor)*
aisle *(gangway between seats)* — isle *(an island)*   I'll *(I will)*
ascent *(going up)* — assent *(to agree)*
already *(previous)* — all ready *(all are ready)*
aloud *(say out loud)* — allowed *(to be permitted)*
altar *(church furniture)* — alter *(to change)*
ant *(insect)* — aunt *(relative)*
ate *(did eat)* — eight *(the number 8)*
are *(plural of **is** or **am**)* — our *(belonging to)*
ball *(round object)* — bawl *(to cry)*
bare *(naked)* — bear *(animal)*
be *(exist)* — bee *(insect)*
beat *(whip)* — beet *(vegetable)*
been *(past tense of be)* — bin *(box)*
berry *(small juicy fruit)* — bury *(put/hide underground)*
blue *(the colour)* — blew *(past tense blow)*
brake *(stop)* — break *(smash)*
bye *(farewell)* — buy *(purchase)* by *(near)*
clothes *(clothing)* — close (shut)   cloze *(a test)*
cereal *(breakfast food* — serial *(one after another)*
compliment *(comment nicely)* — complement *(make complete)*
creek *(a stream)* — creak *(a grating sound)*
currant *(small dried fruit)* — current *(happening now)*

deer *(animal)*   dear *(a greeting or loved one)*
descent *(going down)*   dissent *(disagree)*
desert *(barren land/abandon)*   dessert *(pudding)*
device *(a made thing)*   devise *(plan or invent)*
die *(singular of dice)*   die (to expire)   dye *(colour)*
draft *(first writing attempt/*   draught *(a current or air)*
        to draw someone in)
enquire *(ask a general question)* inquire *(request information)*
fair *(honest or carnival)*   fare *(cost of transport)*
feet *(plural of foot)*   feat *(accomplishment)*
farther *(to go further)*   father *(a male parent)*
find *(to discover)*   fined (a *money penalty)*
flower *(bloom)*   flour *(milled grain)*
four *(the number 4)*   for *(in favour of)*   fore *(front)*
groan *(unpleasant sound)*   grown *(increase in size)*
great *(large)*   grate *(to grind)*
guessed *(past tense of guess)*   guest *(visitor)*
heard *(listen)*   herd *(a group of animals)*
heel *(back of foot)*   heal *(to repair)* he'll *(he will)*
here *(this place)*   hear *(listen)*
hi *(hello)*   high *(opposite of low)*
hole *(opening)*   whole *(complete)*
horse *(animal)*   hoarse *(husky voice)*
I *(pronoun)*   eye *(organ of sight)* aye *(yes)*
in *(opposite of out)*   inn *(hotel)*
its *(possessive noun)*   it's *(it is)*
knot *(tied together/wood mark)* not *(in no way)*
led *(guided)*   lead *(metal)*
loan *(something borrowed)*   lone *(single)*
made *(manufactured)*   maid *(servant)*
mail *(post sent and received)*   male *(gender for a man)*
main *(most important)*   mane *(hair)*
medal *(an honour or award)*   meddle *(to interfere)*
meet *(greet)*   meat *(beef, pork etc.)*
might *(may or strength)*   mite *(small insect)*

missed *(failed to achieve)*   mist *(fog)*
morn *(early part of day)*   mourn *(to grieve)*
morning *(before noon)*   mourning *(grieving)*
past *(past time)*   passed *(past tense of pass)*
need *(require)*   knead *(mix with hands)*
new *(not old)*   knew *(remembered)*
night *(evening)*   knight *(a warrior)*
no *(negative)*   know *(familiar with)*
oh *(exclamation)*   owe *(be indebted)*
one *(the number 1)*   won *(triumphed)*
or *(conjunction)*   oar *(of a boat)*
our *(possessive pronoun)*   hour *(sixty minutes)*
pair *(two of a kind)*   pare *(peel)*   pear *(fruit)*
pause *(to wait)*   paws *(animal feet)*
peace *(tranquil)*   piece *(part)*
plane *(flat surface)*   plain *(simple)*
practise *(verb - do repeatedly)*   practice *(noun – do regularly)*
precede *(in front of or before)*   proceed *(to go on)*
profit (money made selling)   prophet *(teacher/someone who foretells the future)*

principal *(headteacher)*   principle *(a rule)*
rain *(precipitation)*   reign *(royal rule)*
    rein (*harness*)

read *(to peruse)*   reed *(a plant)*
real *(genuine)*   reel *(spool)*
red *(colour)*   read *(perused)*
right *(correct)*   write *(inscribe)*
road *(street)*   rode *(transport)*
    rowed *(as in boats)*

sale *(bargain prices)*   sail *(travel by boat)*
see *(visualize)*   sea *(ocean)*
scene *(a view or image)*   seen *(past tense of see)*
seem *(appear to be)*   seam *(joining mark)*
sell *(exchange for money)*   cell *(prison/tiny living thing)*
sent *(did send)*   cent *(money)*   scent *(odour)*

shoe *(foot covering)* — shoo *(drive away)*
side *(flank)* — sighed *(audible breath)*
so *(in that order)* — sew *(mend)*   sow *(plant)*
some *(portion)* — sum *(total)*
son *(male offspring)* — sun *(star)*
steal *(rob)* — steel *(metal)*
stationery *(writing materials)* — stationary *(not moving)*
steel *(metal)* — steal *(take without permission)*
tail *(animal's appendage)* — tale *(story)*
they're *(they are)* — their *(pronoun)*   there *(place)*
through *(finished)* — threw *(tossed)*
two *(the number 2)* — to *(towards)*   too *(also)*
toe *(on foot)* — tow *(to pull)*
told *(informed)* — tolled *(rang)*
wander *(to move)* — wonder *(enquire/think about)*
wandered *(move around)* — wondered *(show curiosity)*
way *(road/path)* — weigh *(to measure)*
we *(pronoun)* — wee *(small)*
weather *(climate)* — whether *(if)*
week *(seven days)* — weak *(not strong)*
where *(what place)* — wear *(have on)*
who's *(who is)* — whose *(possessive of who)*
wood *(of a tree)* — would *(willing to)*
which *(what one)* — witch *(magical woman)*
wait *(to pause)* — weight *(measurement)*
who's *(who is/who has)* — whose *(belonging to someone)*
your *(possessive pronoun)* — you're *(you are)*

HYPERBOLES AND EXAGGERATION

Everyone like to exaggerate a little bit sometimes, don't they?
Hyperboles *are just an extreme method of exaggeration used for even greater effect when making a point...*

Examples of hyperboles

I'm so tired I could sleep for a week.
I've told you like a million times to tidy your room.
It's raining cats and dogs.
I'm so hungry I could eat a horse.
Her smile was as wide as the River Thames.
His voice was as loud as a lion's roar.
The movie was out of this world.
This is the worst day ever!
I've laughed so hard; I thought my sides would split.
It was so quiet in class you could've heard a pin drop.
He's got a heart as big as Liverpool.
I've been waiting forever!
I was so embarrassed I thought I'd die of shame.
He'd heard the excuse given hundreds of times before.
The news spread like wildfire through the school.
I thought I might explode with excitement!
Church was so boring I thought the world had stopped turning.
Her eyes grew as wide as saucers at the sight before her.
She'd a mountain of homework to complete over the weekend.
Time stood still for them all.
His screams were so high-pitched they could've shattered glass.
Mum's patience was so thin I thought it would eventually snap – and it did!
I was so happy that I felt like I was floating on air.
It looked as though she was carrying the whole weight of the world on her young shoulders.
His bedroom looked like a bomb had hit it.

HYPHENS

*Hyphens are used to join two words together, often to describe a **noun**. They can help to avoid confusion when we write sentences.*

able-bodied	high-tech	round-trip
anti-theft	ill-timed	runner-up
brother-in-law	in-depth	self-service
call-up	know-it-alls	short-change
check-in	large-scale	single-minded
clean-cut	left-handed	strong-arm
daughter-in-law	life-size	tie-break
double-cross	low-grade	tip-off
empty-handed	low-key	toss-up
ex-husband	middle-aged	two-thirds
face-saving	mother-in-law	ultra-violet
father-in-law	near-sighted	U-turn
follow-up	non-starter	walk-on
front-runner	off-peak	warm-up
get-together	off-site	well-being
good-looking	old-fashioned	well-known
habit-forming	one-sided	worn-out
half-witted	passer-by	x-ray
half-hearted	quick-witted	work-shy
high-spirited	word-of-mouth	one-way

*You can also add two words together to create your own **hyphenated words** or **phrases** (also known as **Kennings** as in **Kennings poems**) by adding a **noun** to a **verb** or by joining two **nouns** together for extra effect.*

*Kennings were originally used by the Anglo-Saxons to name a **person**, **place**, **event** or **object** indirectly.*

Examples
blood-curdling, bone-house, ear-piercing, ear-splitting, gut-wrenching, heart-breaking, jaw-breaker, life-giving, mind-blowing, nail-biting, sky-scraping, spine-tingling, sword-slasher

IDIOMS

*Idioms are phrases which mean something different from its real or literal meaning. For example, were we to say **it's raining cats and dogs** we don't actually mean there are pets falling from the sky, just that it's raining heavily - although a lot of **idioms** are actually based on real or historic events...*

(SEE ALSO METAPHORS AND HYPERBOLES)

A right piece of work - *means they're difficult, nasty or sometimes a little tricky to understand.*

Barking up the wrong tree - *means you're looking for something in the wrong place or blaming the wrong person.*

Bigger fish to fry – *means having more important or pressing matters to attend to.*

Bird's-eye view - *means you're seeing things from high up and getting a clearer picture of everything.*

Bite the bullet - *means to face a difficult situation with courage.*

Break a leg – *actors say this instead of saying 'Good luck'.*

Bring home the bacon - *means to earn money to provide for your family.*

Butter someone up – *means to give compliments to someone to make them like you or get what you want from them.*

Cost an arm and a leg - *means something is/was very expensive.*

Couch potato – *means someone who likes to sit around and watch TV instead of being active.*

Cry over spilled milk - *means not getting upset about something that's already happened and can't be changed.*

Don't count your chickens before they hatch – *means not to plan on things which might not happen.*

Egghead - *a playful term for a person who is highly intelligent.*

First come, first served – *means whoever arrives first gets the first choice/first thing on offer.*

Full of beans - *means they're full of energy and enthusiasm.*

Get cold feet - *means feeling scared and unsure about going through with something.*

Head in the clouds – *means someone is daydreaming or not paying full attention.*
Hit the hay/hit the sack - *means to go to bed.*
Hit the nail on the head - *means to say or describe something exactly right.*
Hold your horses - *means to slow down or wait a minute.*
In a pickle - *means you're in a difficult or tricky situation.*
Let the cat out of the bag - *means accidentally saying or revealing something before you're supposed to.*
Like a bull in a china shop - *means moving around clumsily.*
Like a fish out of water - *means someone who's in a situation that feels strange or uncomfortable for them.*
Like two peas in a pod - *means people who are very similar or are extremely close friends.*
On cloud nine - *means you're extremely happy,*
On the same page - *means you both understand and agree about something with someone else.*
Piece of cake – *means something is very easy.*
Pulling your leg – *means having a laugh or a joke or teasing someone.*
Six of one, half a dozen of the other - *means the two options are basically the same as six and half-a-dozen are the same amount.*
Spill the beans - *means to accidentally reveal information that was supposed to be a secret.*
The icing on the cake – *means a situation which was good/bad enough on its own but something else comes along and makes it even better/worse.*
Three strikes and you're out – *means no more chances if you fail or do something wrong again.*
Two heads are better than one – *means that when you work with someone, your ideas can become even better.*
Under the weather - *means not feeling well.*
When pigs fly/When hell freezes over – *means something can't or won't happen as it's impossible.*

IMPERATIVE - *BOSSY* - VERBS

*Imperative or bossy verbs are normally used in **command sentences** which give instructions or tells someone how to do something...*

Examples of imperative verbs
add chop cut explain fetch get go hold hand jump measure move open order pick place pour push put set slice stand stop turn use wash

Now, see how putting put an ***imperative*** or ***bossy* verb** at the beginning of a sentence immediately turns it into a ***command sentence*** in the examples below...

Add more water.
Chop into tiny pieces.
Clean your room!
Cut!
Do as you're told!
Do your homework.
Explain yourself.
Fetch me a cloth.
Get out!
Give me that book!
Go - now!
Hand me the phone.
Hold on for a second.
Jump!
Measure carefully.
Move slowly.
Open up – police!
Stop talking to me.
Stand and deliver!
Take the bins out, please.
Turn left at the lights.
Push!

JUXTAPOSITIONS

Juxtapositions are when you deliberately place two opposing things together to deliberately see the contrast between them. If used well, they can be very effective, especially when writing poetry.

You will also come across *juxtapositions* when talking to people on a daily basis, especially when you're comparing something to something else...

Examples of juxtapositions:

all shapes and sizes
blow hot and cold
black and white
fire and ice
good and evil
great and small
heaven and hell
love and war
light and darkness
old and new
sweet and sour
take the rough with the smooth
the best of times...the worst of times
urban and rural
young and old
war and peace

METAPHORS

Metaphors are a literary device which compares something directly to something else in order to create a resemblance to it...
(SEE ALSO IDIOMS AND HYPERBOLES)

a cloud of fear hovered over them – *showing someone was frightened*
a giant in their field – *someone who is great at what they do*
a guiding light – *someone setting an example/showing the way*
a knight in shining armour – *saving someone/doing something heroic*
a night owl – *someone who stays awake at night*
a wild-goose chase – *a pointless or hopeless waste of time*
an open book – *having nothing to hide*
bent out of shape – *describing someone who is angry*
bite the bullet - *do something unpleasant against their will*
by the skin of your teeth - *manage to do something just in time*
carry a torch for someone – *have feelings towards someone who doesn't feel the same about you*
caught red-handed – *found doing something illegal or forbidden*
cover your bases - *consider all possible outcomes*
cut corners - *do something poorly to save time or money*
cut them some slack – *forgive someone's mistake or fault*
drowning in grief – *overwhelmed with sorrow*
get out of hand – *something becomes out of control*
go back to the drawing board - *start something over again*
having kittens – *worry excessively/unnecessarily about something*
heart of glass – *being of a fragile nature*
heart of gold - *someone who's very kind and generous*
heart of stone – *having a cruel or stern nature*
her cheeks were on fire – *she was embarrassed*
her heart melts – *loving, sympathetic or compassionate*
her heart sank – *feeling of loss, sorrow or dread*
hit the books – *to study*

on the ball – *be alert or to react quickly*
it's all gone pear-shaped – *it's all gone wrong.*
it's showtime – *time to do something important*
like herding cats – *a difficult or frustrating task or situation*
mark my words – *someone makes a prediction they're certain will come true*
miss the boat – *let an opportunity go due to inattention or lack of time or effort*
more than you can shake a stick at – *more than you can handle*
no room to swing a cat – *tiny room or area*
no skin off my nose – *you don't care about something*
pull someone's leg – *gently lie to someone as a way of teasing them*
speak of the devil – *talking about someone as they join you*
splitting hairs – *paying too much attention to unimportant details*
step up to the plate – *take action when needed.*
they're a machine – *someone driven or relentless*
the curtains of life fell – *means that a person's life is over*
the elephant in the room – *something everybody is thinking but nobody is saying*
the moon was a broken bangle – *half-moon*
there's a rat among us – *someone who has betrayed*
they think the world revolves around them – *a self-centred person or behaviour*
this room's a pigsty – *messy and untidy*
wears their heart on their sleeve – *shows their feelings openly*
work was a nightmare – *a bad day at work.*
wrap your head around something – *take time to understand something difficult or hard-to-believe*
you're a shining star – *someone who inspires others*
you're just nitpicking – *someone highlighting tiny faults in someone else*
your words cut like a knife – *you've hurt someone with what you've said.*

MNEMONICS

*Mnemonics are a technique which can be used to help us remember certain things. They can exist as songs, **acronyms** or rhymes. **Mnemonics** are also great at helping you to remember tricky spellings. Have a go at making up some of your own like the examples below...*

An island **is land** surrounded by water *(island)*
Big **E**lephants **C**an **A**lways **U**nderstand **S**mall **E**lephants. *(because)*
Can't **O**pen **M**y **E**yes. *(come)*
Dad **o**nly **e**ats **s**ardines. *(does)*
Find a **fri**end when **FRI**day **END**s. *(friend)*
Have a **pie**ce of the **pie**. *(piece)*
Here? **Where**? **There**! Every**where**! *(Here/There/Where)*
I saw an **ad** for a **dress** at this address. *(address)*
I've **G**ot **H**airy **T**oes. *(words with -IGHT in them e.g. Light, Fight, Right, Might, Sight Bright)*
Laughing **a**nts **u**nderstand **g**reen **h**ornets. *(laugh)*
Never beli**e**ve a **lie**. *(believe)*
Never **E**at **C**risps - **E**at **S**alad **S**andwiches **A**nd **R**emain **Y**oung. *(necessary)*
Oh, **U** **L**ucky **D**uck! *(words with -OULD in them e.g. Could, would, should etc.)*
Only **C**ats' **E**yes **A**re **N**arrow. *(ocean)*
People **E**at **O**range **P**eelings **L**ike **E**lephants. *(people)*
Rhythm **H**elps **Y**ou **M**ake **Y**our **T**wo **H**ips **M**ove. *(rhythm)*
Sailing **A**cross **I**cy **L**akes. *(sail)*
Silly **A**unts **I**n **D**resses. *(said)*
That **liar** looks fami**liar**. *(familiar)*
The **CIA** has special agents. *(special)*
The **desert** is sandy but a **dessert** is sweetly sweet. *(desert or dessert)*
There's **a rat** in separate. *(separate)*
You **hear** with your **ear**. *(hear)*
You need **to get her** to be **together**. *(together)*

MODAL VERBS

*A **modal verb** is a special type of verb which alters or affects other **verbs** in a sentence. They are usually used to show the level of possibility, to indicate ability, to show obligation or to give permission. **Modal verbs** behave differently from ordinary **verbs** as they can't work on their own without have another **verb** in the sentence for it to make complete sense to the reader...*

Examples of modal verbs

allowed, allowed to, can, cannot, could, could not, have, have not, have to, may, may not, might, might not, must, must not, need, need to, ought, ought not, shall, shall not, should, should not, will be able to, will have to, will not be able to, will not have to, will, will not, would, would not

Examples of modal verbs you can use to show ability:
***Can** I try that again, please?*
*"We **could** always skip back in time," smiled Slipp.*
*"Poppy Copperthwaite **cannot** spellcast," sighed Humphry.*

Examples of modal verbs you can use to give an instruction, to give advice or to state an obligation:
*Children **must** always attend school.*
*You **should** always wash your hands after sneezing.*
*She **ought to** know how to do that by now.*

Examples of modal verbs you can use to indicate possibility:
*I **will** come back for you, that's a promise.*
*We **shall** have our revenge on the humans....*
*If we're lucky, it **might** snow tomorrow.*

Examples of modal verbs you can use to ask/give permission:
*You **can** come out now, no one's looking...*
***Could** you pass me the salt please?*
***May** I ask why I can't go to my friend's house tonight?*

NOUNS – COMMON NOUNS

*A **common noun** is a word used for the general name of something, such as a **person**, **place**, **thing** or **object**. e.g. **city**, **apple**, **hoop** and **doctor**.*

Examples of common nouns
airport beach bear bike car cat chair child church cup customer doctor dog employee fish ground horse lion monkey mountain park pavement person phone pig rabbit road school ship shop singer snake table teacher television tiger tree water

NOUNS – COLLECTIVE NOUNS

*A **collective noun** is a type of **noun** used to show a group of people, animals or objects. e.g. **gang**, **swarm**, **crowd**, **pair**, **group** etc. Some **collective nouns** are general and refer to many things whilst others have **specific** uses such as **flock** which refers to a group of birds.*

Examples of general collective nouns
band bunch couple crew crowd group gang pair team

Examples of specific collective nouns

an army of ants	a hive of bees
a basket of fruit	a horde of savages
a batch of bread	a host of angels
a battery of guns	a library of books
a block of flats	a line of kings
a board of directors	a murder of crows
a body of men	a murder of ravens
a book of notes	a pack of thieves
a bouquet of flowers	a pack of wolves
a broad of chickens	a plague of locusts
a bunch of keys	a pride of lions
a bundle of sticks	a quiver of arrows

a class of students
a cloud of dust
a colony of badgers
a fleet of ships
a flock of seagulls
a forest of trees
a gaggle of geese
a galaxy of stars
a group of islands
a hail of bullets
a hand of bananas
a harvest of wheat
a heap of rubbish
a herd of cattle

a range of mountains
a ream of paper
a reel of film
a regiment of soldiers
a school of whales
a set of clubs
a shoal of fish
a shower of rain
a stack of wood
a string of pearls
a stud of horses
a swarm of bees
a troop of scouts
a wad of notes

NOUNS –
PROPER NOUNS / CAPITALISATION

*Proper nouns are the specific name of a **person, place** or **object** and **MUST** always have a **capital letter** for the **whole name** of them/it (e.g. the Eiffel Tower). However, as always, there are rules when adding **capital letters** to **proper nouns** as book and newspaper titles, headlines/sub-headings and bylines also use **capitals**..*

Knowing which types of words to capitalise is the most important thing to remember as there are three rules you must always follow and use a capital letter for when writing:

1. *A capital letter or proper nouns*
2. *A capital letter or the pronoun I*
3. *A capital letter or the first word in a sentence or the opening or closing line in a letter (e.g. Dear Bob, Yours sincerely, etc.)*

Using capitals for **proper nouns** is where the greatest confusion often lies. Some words, like my name *Jonas Lane*, are always capitalised.

However, many others only need **capitals** in certain situations and are written using **lowercase** letters instead. For example, the directions **north, south, east** and **west** are normally written in **lowercase** but are capitalised when part of a place name.

e.g. *South Africa, West Ham, East of England, North Korea* etc.

So, what words need to be capitalised then, Jonas? I hear you ask. Well, let me try and make this as simple possible for you, dear reader, in this easy-to-remember guide...

A person's name - The first and last names of a person's full name, along with any middle or **hyphenated** names are always capitalised, along with initials, nicknames or **prefixes, suffixes** or **abbreviations** such as *Dr. Snr. Jr. OBE* etc.

Examples

J.K. Rowling, Edgar Allan Poe, Martin Luther King Jr., Taylor Swift, Dr. Foster, King Charles III, Dwayne 'The Rock' Johnson
Honorifics like *Mr, Mrs, Master, Miss and Ms.* are also always capitalised.

Names which have been abbreviated into acronyms – These too use *capitals* when letters are used to abbreviate a whole name with each one then being a capital letter.

Examples

*QPR (**Q**ueens **P**ark **R**angers), GMT (**G**reenwich **M**ean **T**ime)*
*WHO (**W**orld **H**ealth **O**rganization) RAF (**R**oyal **A**ir **F**orce)*
*HRH (**H**is/**H**er **R**oyal **H**ighness)*

The name of a place – When writing the name of somewhere you must use *capital letters* for the whole name.

Examples

Liverpool, New York City, Bedford, Earth, Lake Bled, Outer Mongolia etc.

The names of countries, nationalities, and languages – These are also capitalised as country names are all classed as places. In addition to this, people who live there and the *adjective* form of their culture must be shown in *capitals* too (this includes their languages).

Examples

Italy, the Italian football team, Italian food such as pizza etc.

The names of days, months or holidays – The names of days and months must always be capitalised as they all are proper nouns too.

Examples
Sunday, Monday, Tuesday etc., January, February, March etc.
However, if a word like *day* or *month* is used generally in a sentence, then they must not be capitalised unless they are part of a holiday name, commemorative day or month when they become a ***proper noun*** and should also then be capitalised.

Examples
Mother's Day, Boxing Day, Christmas Day, Good Friday, August Bank Holiday, Black History Month

The names of companies, organisations and institutions - The names of brands, companies and other large groups like hospitals etc. are also proper nouns, though some small words used - like ***determiners*** and ***prepositions*** - may still be written in lowercase.

Examples
Barclays Bank, Camestone School, Hogwarts School of Witchcraft and Wizardry, Liverpool Football Club, Tesco, Great Ormond Street Hospital, Mercedes Benz etc.

Names which are historical - Names which include descriptive words often follow the title capitalisation rules where prominent words are capitalised, but words like **determiners** and ***prepositions*** aren't.

Examples
Catherine of Aragon, Henry the Eighth, Vlad the Impaler, Ivan the Terrible, William of Orange, the Duke of Wellington etc.

The names of historical eras, periods and events – You also use ***capital letters*** for these when referring to them by their specific name but not when using them in general terms.

If a time period is named after a ***proper noun***, remember to capitalise the ***proper noun*** too. Often the word for the period is ***capitalised*** but on other occasions you may find that it's written in lowercase as in the *Victorian age,* though the *Victorian Era* is written in capitals for some reason!

Examples
Middle Ages, Boxer Rebellion, War of the Roses, Tudor England, Ancient Greece, the Roman Empire, Ancient Egypt, World War II

However, do not capitalise the names of centuries because they are too broad. e.g. *the nineteenth century.*

The names of publications and titles – This is where a lot of capitalisation mistakes come from. The title of any piece of work - books, newspapers, magazines, movies, songs, poems, graphic novels etc.- requires capitalisation, but, as in other examples we've already come across, only certain words in the title are **capitalised.**

So, exactly which words need to be capitalised in titles, Jonas?
Well, I was just about to come to that...
As with sentences, the first word in a title is always capitalised. ***Nouns, pronouns, verbs, adjectives***, and ***adverbs*** all need to have capitals in titles as well, whilst small words like ***determiners*** and ***preposition***s are usually written in ***lowercase*** unless they're the first word in a title.

Examples
The Sunday Times, The Lion, the Witch and the Wardrobe, Harry Potter and the Chamber of Secrets, Bohemian Rhapsody, The Lord of the Rings, The Nightmare Before Christmas, The Owl and the Pussycat etc.

With **_headings_** and **_subheadings_**, remember to always use the **_sentence case_** (that means you capitalise the first letter and any words that would use capitals in a normal sentence). Also avoid using all capital letters, as well as putting a full stop at the end. So, all clear on when to use capital letters? Well, just to confuse matters even more, there are other instances where other words are sometimes capitalised...

Names used for family members – Now this can be a confusing topic. Family member names like _dad, mum, auntie,_ or _uncle_ can be both **_proper nouns_** or **_common nouns_** depending on how and when you use them. The easiest way to remember the difference is if you are using them as a **_proper noun,_** then always use a capital.

Examples
**Aunt** Sheila is my favourite relative.
Can I go to the cinema, **Dad**?
Thank you for the pocket money, **Nan**.

However, if you're writing them as a **_common noun_**, a capital letter is then not needed...

Examples
My **aunt** is my favourite relative.
I'll have to ask my **dad** if I can go to the cinema.
I was given some pocket money by my **nan**.

The names of the seasons – Generally, the seasons of _spring, summer, autumn_ and _winter_ are not capitalised so are written in lowercase like other **_common nouns_**.

Examples
We had a really wet **summer** but a baking hot **spring** and **autumn** last year.

However, if a season is used as part of a title, then they become part of a *proper noun* and are therefore capitalised.

Examples
Spring Bank Holiday, *Autumn* term, *Summer* Season 24/25

Names which are either job titles or positions of importance – Job titles, positions, or honorifics – a form of address showing importance or respect like *Professor or Doctor* - are sometimes capitalised and sometimes written in lowercase.

However, when these titles are used as part of a *proper name*, they are always capitalised and when they refer to a general job title or position they are then written in lowercase.

Examples
Sir David Attenborough is one of the greatest broadcasters this country has ever had.
This way please, *sir*.
Professor Minerva McGonagall taught Transfiguration, one of the most dangerous types of magic studies at Hogwarts. She was Harry's favourite **professor** there.
President Donald Trump was the worst **president** ever...

NOUNS - ABSTRACT NOUNS

Abstract nouns are used to describe something which exists but we cannot see or touch e.g. **love, dream, fear** or **hope**. We can organise them like this...

Examples of abstract nouns you could use to show feelings or emotions: amazement anger anxiety apprehension concern confusion delight despair disappointment disbelief doom dread excitement friendship grief happiness joy misery pain passion pleasure pride regret relaxation relief romance sadness satisfaction silliness sorrow surprise thrill tiredness trepidation uncertainty worry

Examples of abstract nouns you could use to show human qualities: ambition awe beauty bravery brilliance calmness charity compassion confidence courage curiosity dedication determination ego elegance enthusiasm envy evil faithfulness fear generosity goodness graciousness hatred helpfulness helplessness honesty honour hope humility humour insanity intelligence jealousy kindness love loyalty maturity patience power self-control self-discipline sensitivity strength stupidity sympathy talent tolerance trust warmth weakness wisdom wit

Examples of abstract nouns you could use to show thoughts and ideas: adventure consideration crime democracy education experience failure faith forgiveness fragility idea imagination improvement independence justice knowledge law life loss luck mercy need opportunity peace poverty reality thought truth victory wealth

Other examples of abstract nouns you could use in your writing: ability belief chaos comfort curse death deceit dream energy favoritism gossip grace hearsay laughter memory movement nightmare omen opinion premonition principle reason rumour shock sleep visions wishes

Now a question I'm always asked in class - is a word like *happy* an abstract noun? Well, let's try it out in a sentence shall we...

Jonas felt extremely happy as it was his birthday.

In the above sentence, the word **happy** is describing *Jonas,* which is a **proper noun,** so *happy* is an **adjective** when used in this way. For **happy** to be used as an **abstract noun** you must add the **suffix -ness** to it so that it becomes the word **happiness** instead.

This you can also do with other adjectives in exactly the same way, changing them into **abstract nouns** too.

Examples
empty becomes *emptiness*
good becomes *goodness*
kind becomes *kindness*
lonely becomes *loneliness*
mad becomes *madness*
sad becomes *sadness*

NOUN PHRASES

*A **noun phrase** is a group of words or a short sentence which contains a **noun or a pronoun** along with other words that describes or changes the **noun**.*

Examples of simple noun phrases
The fox.
A lion.
Some strawberries.

EXPANDED NOUN PHRASES

*Expanded noun phrases simply add more detail to the **noun** by adding one or more **adjectives** - as well as other word classes - to provide extra information to the reader.*

Examples of expanded nouns phrases
The sly fox.
A dangerous lion.
Some delicious strawberries.

An **expanded noun phrase** can also add extra detail by saying **where** a **noun** is. e.g. *A dangerous lion roams **across** the African plains.*

You can then expand it even further by adding a **relative clause** using **with, who, which,** or **that** to provide even more detail...

*A dangerous lion, **with** enormous teeth, roams across the African plains.*
*A dangerous lion, **who** is very hungry, roams across the African plains.*
*A dangerous lion, **which** is the largest member of the cat family, roams across the African plains.*
*A dangerous shark, **that** can run extremely fast, roams across the African plains.*

ONOMATOPOEIA

Onomatopoeia are words which often sound like what they mean. e.g. **thud, ouch oi, crash, bang** *and* **buzz** *(these are also known as* **interjections**)*.. Most though simply show the noise or sound in a sentence. Try using some* **onomatopoeia** *in your own writing...*

Examples of onomatopoeia

*As a child, Mason used to be afraid of things which went **bump** in the night.*

*The sound of pots and pans **clanging** in the kitchen alerted her to the intruder.*

*'Tlot-Tlot' went the horse's hooves as they **clip-clopped** over the cobblestones of the old inn yard.*

*Tristan's blade fell to the ground with a tremendous **clatter**.*

*He felt the **crunch** of bone and cartilage as his fist met the nose of the man stood before him.*

*Poppy winced at the sound of the enormous **belch** which suddenly erupted from the depths of Humphry's bloated stomach.*

*Zac could feel the tension build inside him as Miss Fletcher's high-heels **clacked** on the wooden floor as she approached him.*

*The **squeak** of Slipp's shoes immediately awoke the guard as he tried to escape the tower.*

*Watson began to **meow** loudly as the strange figure walked past the window.*

*The Sárkány's head made a sickening **thud** as it fell to the floor.*

*Wilde smiled at the sound of the sonic **boom** the Icarus made as it parted the heavy storm clouds around them.*

*Alex and Georgie heard the Time Skipper **hum** loudly.*

*A sudden **creak** from the stair beneath his feet caused Josh to stop momentarily, afraid that he'd been caught red-handed.*

*The **ticking** of the clock seemed to be in perfect time with that of Magda's heartbeat.*

*Nona's bag landed with a **thump** against her bedroom door.*

OXYMORONS

Oxymorons are phrases or *figures of speech* that combine two words or ideas which seem to be completely opposite to one another to create a brand-new meaning. They are a great way to play with your language skills when writing...

Examples of oxymorons

act naturally	a loud whisper	a numb feeling
a sure bet	a true story	a blind eye
accidentally on purpose		alone in a crowd
almost done	almost there	an honest crook
an open secret	another one	awfully delicious
awfully good	awfully nice	bad luck
bittersweet	calculated risk	clearly confused
clearly misunderstood	clever fool	crash landing
deafening silence	distant relative	dull pain
deliberate mistake		educated guess
fine mess	free slave	front end
half full	ill health	immediate future
inside out	least favourite	live recording
living dead	loose fit	love-hate
midnight sun	minor disaster	much less
near miss	never again	old news
once again	one pair	only choice
organised chaos	pretty ugly	poor little rich girl
quiet noise	random order	real-life fairy tale
restless sleep	sad smile	same difference
science fiction	second best	seriously funny
sharp curve	short distance	sleepwalk
small world	still moving	sweet misery
sweet sorrow	temporary fix	thinking out loud
tough love	uninvited guest	upside down
unbelievably real	virtual reality	whole piece

PARAGRAPHING

*Paragraphs help to structure your writing as each new **paragraph** starts on a new line. They are groups of **sentences** of various lengths which share a common idea or topic. e.g. You start a new **paragraph** to show that the person, place, time or topic has changed.*

*Paragraphs are also used if the point of view switches from one character to another, whereas in a non-fiction text, they're used when there is usually a common theme. The length of a **paragraph** is based on what the writer is trying to say, meaning once could be as little as one or two sentences if written for impact.*

*As with many other aspects of writing, there are some very important rules to follow when using **paragraphs**...*

Start a new paragraph to help break long narratives up - Instead of writing a long speech delivered by a character, break the narrative into smaller paragraphs to make it easier to read.

"Whilst I appreciate you all applauding," she smiled, "it's really us here at the Valiant who should be showing our gratitude to you dear parents, for raising such gifted and talented children who will no doubt become the next generation of wonderful students to eventually graduate from the academy."

A brief couple of random claps died away as children frowned at their parents before Miss Morgan eventually spoke again.

"However, your work is now done. We thank you for escorting our children here today, but now it's time for you all to leave. Goodbye..."

Start a new paragraph when changing topic — For both fiction and nonfiction, start a new paragraph when a new topic takes place.

"That's just peachy!" Georgie moaned quietly as she pulled on the door handle to confirm what she feared and suspected... She was now locked in the storeroom!

Georgie leant back against the door and slid down it until she reached the ground, not caring that the spilt ale was making her trousers damp, causing the material to stick to her skin.

Start a new paragraph when changing your setting, time jumping or shifting to a new place – When your story shifts from one place or time to another, then start a new paragraph.
The months which followed seemed to drag for Danny, having made up his mind about leaving home for the Valiant. He'd convinced himself that the rest of the family would be fine without him. But the longer it took for enrolment day to arrive, the more doubt crept into his mind.
Eventually, when the clock struck 12pm on December 31st to herald in the new year and a new life for Danny Arter, the teenager now knew that this was the chance he'd always yearned for to escape the life that generations of Arter men had painfully been forced to live.

Start a new paragraph when writing dialogue each time a different character speaks – Speech is one of the easiest rules to remember when paragraphing yet many young writers forget to apply it correctly. Simply put – every time a different character speaks, start a new paragraph. The same rule applies with thoughts.
I wonder if I will see her ever again, Magda thought to herself, looking back at the facility as the truck slowly trundled into the distance as a woman approached her holding a coarse, heavy blanket in her hands.
"Here, child, wear this," the old woman said kindly, "we don't want you catching your death of cold now, do we?"
"Thank you," Magda tiredly replied before sneezing harder than she'd ever done before...

Start a new paragraph when a new person or place is introduced – In much the same way as starting a new paragraph for changing your setting or time, always start a new paragraph when introducing a new person or location.
Rob grinned as he looked at Kat's last message on his phone again.

Almost there, he thought, the excitement he felt mirroring that of the other two hundred and forty-two children, travelling from up and down the country, who were making the same journey as him that cold, January day.
An opportunity given to only a select few...
An opportunity they all felt compelled to take...
An opportunity that would shape their lives, and the destinies of those around them, for years to come...

Almost two hundred and fifty miles away, deep in the deserted Victorian sewers that ran under London's largest glass blowing factory, a lone figure quietly sat.
Waiting...

Start a new paragraph for added effect – Finally, you can always experiment with your writing and add paragraphs for impact, to emphasise an important part in your writing such as a piece of humour or to drive home a message to the reader.

Later that evening, Lenny Chen, flushed from the success of the restaurant's opening night, immediately said 'Yes' saying it was too good an opportunity for Lexi to miss.
But - in reality - he saw it more as an opportunity for him to save money with his daughter living away from home. Money that could be spent on the odd bet here, or there, now and again...
And again...
And again...

PARENTHESIS

*Parenthesis is when you add either a **word, phrase** or **sentence** to your writing to provide extra information or it can also be used as an afterthought, using either a pair of **brackets**, a pair of **commas** or a pair of **dashes**. The additional information **parenthesis** gives the **sentence** is known as a **relative** or **embedded clause** because if you were to take it away, the rest of the **sentence** – the **main clause** – would still make sense without them...*

How writers choose to punctuate their **relative/embedded clause** is purely down to their own personal preference but there are some factors to consider when choosing which one to use...

Adding parenthesis using a pair of commas – Your *relative clause* will look like it is part or an ordinary sentence but the *commas* could then easily be confused with other commas that are also in the sentence for entirely different purposes.
Later that week, Poppy Copperthwaite, the heir to the Majeek throne, would star in a televised broadcast to celebrate her Coming of Mage.

Adding parenthesis using a pair of dashes – Using *dashes* will ensure your *parenthesis* easily stands out in your sentence but may make your **relative clause** then seem a little stark...
Later that week, Poppy Copperthwaite - the heir to the Majeek throne - would star in a televised broadcast to celebrate her Coming of Mage.

Adding parenthesis using a pair of brackets ( ) - Again your parenthesis will be clearly seen but **brackets** can make your writing look a little too informal when using them..
Later that week, Poppy Copperthwaite (the heir to the Majeek throne) would star in a televised broadcast to celebrate her Coming of Mage.

PATHETIC FALLACY / PERSONIFICATION

*Pathetic Fallacy is when a writer gives **human feelings** to something in the natural world (or some part of it) whereas **Personification** means animals, objects or ideas are given **human characteristics**, **actions** or **emotions**. Be careful not to mix the two terms up...*

Examples of pathetic fallacy
*The **friendly sun smiled** brightly down on them.*
*The sky outside was as black as his heart, **weeping its bitter tears**.*
***Fear ran through her veins as cold as the snow** which fell.*
*Zac felt as **miserable** as the weather outside was.*
*The **angry storm raged** above their heads.*

Examples of personification
*After the tragic news, **the whole world weeps** as we do.*
*The hairs on the back of his neck **stood** on end.*
*Suddenly, the tornado **swallowed up** everything in its path.*
*Her heart **danced** merrily when she saw him.*
*Beneath their wet feet, the floorboards **groaned** loudly.*
*As the sky darkened, the thunder **announced** the storm's arrival.*
*Wilde ignored the door's **angry protests** as it slowly opened.*
*The trees' shadows **painted** the frosted ground around them.*
*There, **stood** at the top of the hill, was Slipp Manor in all its glory.*
*Georgie smiled as the Time Skipper **growled** into life.*
*She screamed as she looked down into the **yawning** chasm.*
*"No, I shouldn't..." Alex sighed, trying to ignore the chocolate cheesecake that was **begging** him to eat it.*
*Up above him, a nightingale loudly **sang** a sad melody.*

PERSUASIVE LANGUAGE

*Persuasive language can be used to convince readers of your opinion or point of view. Used well, it can help to sway them to agree with you. You can vary the **persuasive language** you use dependent on what you are writing, who your audience is or your purpose and reason for writing.*

Examples of sentence starters you could use for persuasive introductions: I think... I am sure that... I feel that... It is certain... It is obvious... For this reason... I am writing to... Of course... In the same way... On this occasion...On the other hand... In this instance... In this situation...

Examples of sentence starters you could use to help make your point: Firstly... Secondly... Furthermore... In addition... Also... Finally.. Likewise... Besides... Again... Moreover... Similarly... Surely... Certainly... Specifically...

Examples of sentence starters you could use to give extra detail: For example... In fact... For instance... As evidence... In support of this...To support this...You can see that... As illustrated by...As seen in...

Examples of words you could include to help further illustrate your point of view or argument: such as... reasons.. unfair... arguments... for... against... pros... cons...

Examples of sentence starters you could use to end your persuasive piece or to summarise all the points you've made: For these reasons... In summary... As you can see... In other words... On the whole... In short... Without a doubt... To sum up... Undoubtedly...

PREPOSITIONS

*Prepositions are words that tell you **where** or **when** something is in relation to something else. Examples of **prepositions** include words like **after, before, on, under, inside** and **outside**...*

Prepositions of location and place - These prepositions give the reader more information about where something *is*.

Examples
*Humphry landed heavily **on** his bottom.*
I left my heart in San Fransisco.
*She hid **behind** the curtains.*

Examples of prepositions you could use to indicate location and place: aboard above across against along amid among around at away behind below beneath beside between beyond by close down from in inside into near on onto opposite out outside over under underneath upon

Prepositions of time — These are used to describe when something has happened in the past, something happening now or when something will happen in the future.

Examples:
*The chip shop is closed **on** Sundays.*
*Mobile phones are not allowed **during** the school production.*
*The paper is due **by** Wednesday.*

Examples of prepositions you could use to indicate time: after ago at before by during for from in next on since till to until within

Prepositions of direction and movement — Our final set of prepositions are used to describe the movement of a person or object from one place to another.

They are especially useful when giving directions or describing a location.

Examples:

*The four boys walked **alongside** the old, abandoned railway track, hoping to find adventure.*
*Wilde smiled as she watched the stone she'd thrown skip **across** the surface of the water.*
*Slipp grinned as the stream train went **through** the tunnel.*
*The children ran **away from** the police.*
*Max Power and Will Speed raced **along** the seafront*
*They both sped **around** the corner.*
*Sherwood Holmes charged **down** the hill after them*

Examples of prepositions you could use to indicate direction or movement: above across against along alongside among around/round at away behind below beside between by close from in inside into near next off on onto out outside over past through to toward under underneath up and down

PREPOSITIONAL PHRASES

*Now that you know your **prepositions**, **prepositional phrases** are just groups of words which begin with a **preposition** and end with **a noun, pronoun**, or **noun phrase**. They can be used anywhere in the sentence. (SEE ALSO FRONTED ADVERBIALS AND RELATIVES CLAUSES).*

Examples of prepositional phrases:

Watson hid his favourite toy mouse underneath the sofa.

Under the blood-filled moon stands a castle like no other.

Beside the poisonous river the forest quietly waits...

Beneath the gigantic mountain lies the sleepy village of Mortudore.

Below the violent volcano, the people of Naples go about their normal, everyday lives.

Across the desolate wastelands rests the last hope for all of mankind.

In front of the apocalyptic ocean, next to the white-chalked cliffs, is an abandoned - and some say haunted - lighthouse.

Over the hills and far away lies the mysterious kingdom known only as Unimaginatia.

Beyond the palace gates, life was very different for the princess...

Behind the school was a playground which had been shut and abandoned for many years.

Mrs Jones smiled as she deposited her cheque into her local building society account.

At the foot of the hills, hidden by their shadows, lies a deserted city of forbidden dreams.

Nestling deep in the forest rests the empty city of unfulfilled wishes...

The cinema, which had once seen far better days, was located directly opposite the subway.

I could tell that there was danger nearby by the way that my dog was barking so crazily.

PREFIXES

*Prefixes are groups of letters which - when added to the beginning of a **root word** - change its meaning, often making it an opposite word (**antonym**). Each **prefix** has a meaning of its own whilst some **prefixes** also requires **hyphens**...*

Prefix	Meaning	Examples
anti-	*against/opposed to*	anti-war, anti-racist,
aqua-	*water*	aquanaut, aquarium
aero-	*air or flight*	aerodrome, aeroplanes
audi-	*to hear*	audible, audio
auto-	*self*	autobiography, automobile
de-	*reverse or change*	de-classify, demotivate
dis-	*reverse or remove*	disagree, displeasure,
down-	*reduce or lower*	downgrade, downhearted
extra-	*beyond*	extraordinary, extraterrestrial
hyper-	*extreme*	hyperactive, hypertension
il-, im-,	*not*	illegal, impossible
in-, ir-	*not*	insecure, irregular
inter-	*between*	interactive, international
mega-	*very big, important*	megabyte, mega-deal,
micro-	*small*	microphone, microscope
mid-	*middle*	midnight, mid-October
mis-	*incorrectly, badly*	misaligned, mislead, misspelt
non-	*not*	non-payment, non-smoking
over-	*too much*	overcook, overcharge,
out-	*go beyond*	outdo, out-perform, outrun
post-	*after*	post-election, post-war
pre-	*before*	prehistoric, pre-war
prim-	*first*	prime, primary
pro-	*in favour of*	pro-democracy, pro-choice
re-	*again*	reconsider, redo, rewrite
semi-	*half*	semicircle, semi-retired
sub-	*under, below*	submarine, subterranean
super-	*above, beyond*	super-hero, supermodel

tele-	*at a distance*	television, telepathic
trans-	*across* or *beyond*	transatlantic, transfer
ultra-	*extremely*	ultra-compact, ultrasound
un-	*remove, reverse, not*	undo, unpack, unhappy
under-	*less than, beneath*	undercook, underestimate
up-	*make or move higher*	upgrade, uphill

Below are examples of words using the prefixes you're expected to know before starting secondary school.

Examples of the prefix *un-* which usually means *remove, reverse* or *not*: unable unacceptable unafraid unanswered unanticipated unappealing unaware unbearable unbutton uncertain uncomfortable uncommon unconcerned unconscious unconvinced undamaged undecided undo uneasy unemployed unending uneven unexpected unfair unfamiliar unfit unfollow unfortunately unhappy unhurt unimportant unimpressed uninterested unknown unlawful unlikely unlimited unlocked unpack unpaid unreasonable unsaid unselfish unspoken unstoppable untie untrue unveil unwanted unwrap

Examples of the prefix *de-* which usually means *reverse* or *change*: de-ice deactivate deactivation declutter decode, decoded decommission decompose decomposition deconstruct, decontaminate decontamination decrease, deflate, deflated deflation deflect deform demythologise derail detract

Examples of the prefix *dis-* which usually means *reverse* or *change*: disable disaffected disagree disagreeable disagreement disappear disappoint disarm disassemble discomfort discourage discover discredit disgrace disguise dishonest dishonour dishonourable disinfect disinfected disinterest dislike disloyal disobey disorder disown displace displease displeased displeasure disprove disregard disrespect dissolve distasteful distrust distrustful

Examples of the prefix *mis-* which usually means *incorrectly* or *badly*: misadvise misbehave miscalculate miscarry misfit misfortune misguided mishandle misheard misinterpret misjudge mislead misled misplace misquote misread misspent mistakable mistake mistook mistrust misunderstand misunderstood misuse

Examples of the prefix *re-* which usually means *again* or *back*: re-enter reappear rearrange reassemble recalculate recall recount recreate redecorate rediscover redo regain reiterate rejoice rejoin rekindle remarry reoccupy repeat reread rerecord rerun resell rework rewrite

Examples of the prefix *sub-* which usually means *under* or *below*: subcontinent subcontractor subdivide subdued subheading subject submarine submerge submerse submit subscribe subterranean subtract subtropical subvert subway

Examples of the prefix *im-* which usually means *not*: imbalance immature immeasurable immoral immortal impartial impatient impenetrable imperfect impolite impossible impractical improper

Examples of the prefix *in-* which also usually means *not* as well as *in/into*: inaccurate inadmissible inadvertently incapable incoherent incomparable incompatible incompetent incomplete incomprehensible inconclusive inconsiderate inconvenience incorrect indecisive indefinite independence indescribable indifferent ineffective inequality inevitable inexpensive inexplicable infamous informal inhumane insane insecure invalid

Examples of the prefix *il-* which also usually means *not*: illegal illegible illicit illiteracy illiterate illogical illusion

Examples of the prefix *ir-*... which also usually means *not*: irrational irregular irrelevant irreparable irresistible irresponsible

Examples of the prefix *inter-* which usually means *between* or *among*: interact interactive intercept interchangeable intercity interconnected intercultural interfere interim interlock interlude intermission international interrupt intertwine intervene

Examples of the prefix *super-* which usually means *above* or *beyond*: superficial superfluous superimpose superintendent superior superlative superman supermarket supermodel supernumerary supersonic superstar supervisor

Examples of the prefix anti- which usually means *against* or *opposed to*: antiaircraft antibacterial antibiotic antibody antichrist anticipate anticipation anticlimax anticlockwise, antidepressant antidote antifreeze antifungal antigravity antihero antimatter antioxidant antipathy antiperspirant antiseptic, antisocial antiviral antivirus

Examples of the prefix *auto-* which usually means *self* or *own*: autobiography autocracy autocratic autocue autograph autoimmune automated automatic automation automaton automobile autonomous autopilot

Examples of the prefix *bi-* which usually mean *two*: biangular biannual bicentennial biceps bicycle biennial bifocal bilateral bilingual bimonthly binocular biochemistry biodiversity biofuels biometrics biopsy biotechnology bipartisan biped bipolar bisect bisexual biweekly disorder

Examples of the prefix *aqua-* which usually means *water*: aquamarine aquanaut aquaplane aquarium aquatic aqueduct

Examples of the prefix *aero-* which usually means *air* or *flight*: aerate aerobatics aerodromes aeromedicine aeronautic aeroplanes aerospace

Examples of the prefix *micro-* which usually means *small*: microbe microbiologist microbiology microclimate microcosm microeconomy microfilm micromanage microorganism microphone microprocessor microscope microwave

Examples of the prefix *audi-* which usually means *to hear*: audibility audible audience audiobook audiogram audiology audiometer audiotape audiovisual audition auditorium

Examples of the prefix *trans-* which usually means *across, beyond* or *on the other side of*: transact transatlantic transcontinental transfer transfix transformation transgender transgression transit translate translation translucent transparent transportation

Examples of the prefix *prim-* which usually means *first*: primadonna primal primarily primary primate prime primer primeval primitive primordial primulas

Examples of the prefix *pre-* which usually means before: prearrange precaution precede precious precise predetermine predict preface prefer prefix preheat prejudice preload premature prepaid prepare preschool prescribe present president presume prevent preview previous

Examples of the prefix *tele-* which usually means at a distance: telecast telegenic telegram telegraph telekinesis telemeter telepathy telephone teleport teleportation teleprompter telesales teletape telethon television

PLURALS

*Plural nouns are nouns which refer to more than one **person**, **place**, **thing** or **idea**. Most **singular nouns** can be made **plural** by simply adding a **suffix**, usually –s or –es.*

*However, there are many different rules regarding **pluralisation** depending on what letter a **noun** ends with. Not only that but there are **irregular plural nouns** to remember too!*

These are the main *plural* rules for you to know and remember...

Plural rule number 1 - For most root words you just add *-s*...

Examples
cat becomes *cats*
dog becomes *dogs*
shop becomes *shops*

Plural rule number 2 – If a root word ends with *s*, *sh*, *ch* and *tch* then you add *-es*...

Examples
church becomes *churches*
kiss becomes *kisses*
wish becomes *wishes*
witch becomes *witches*

Plural rule number 3 – Usually, if a root word ends with *f* or *fe* then you add *-ves* although there are a couple of exceptions to the rule...

Examples
hoof becomes *hooves*
leaf becomes *leaves*
life becomes *lives*
knife becomes *knives*
thief becomes *thieves*
wife becomes *wives*

Plural rule number 4 – If a root word ends with a *consonant* followed by the *letter y* you then add *-ies*....

Examples
library becomes *libraries*
story becomes *stories*
theory becomes *theories*

Plural rule number 5 – If a root word ends with a *vowel* followed by the *letter y* you then add *-s*....

Examples
day becomes *days*
key becomes *keys*
toy becomes *toys*

Plural rule number 6 – If a **common** or **concrete noun** ends with a *vowel* followed by the *letter* o you then add *-s*...

Examples
radio becomes *radios*
studio becomes *studios*
torpedo becomes *torpedoes*
video becomes *videos*

Plural rule number 7 – If a *common* or *concrete noun* ends with a *consonant* followed by the *letter o* you then add *-es*...

Examples
domino becomes *dominoes*
hero becomes *heroes*
potato becomes *potatoes*
tomato becomes *tomatoes*
volcano becomes *volcanoes*

WARNING!

As I've already mentioned, there are some *irregular plurals* which do not follow the rules previously advised, so they must be memorised, looked up in the dictionary or the examples listed below referred to...

IRREGULAR PLURALS

*Here are the most common **irregular plurals** for you to know....*

Singular	Plural
child	*children*
die	*dice/dies*
foot	*feet*
goose	*geese*
louse	*lice*
man	*men*
mouse	*mice*
ox	*oxen*
phenomenon	*phenomena*
proof	*proofs*
quiz	*quizzes*
roof	*roofs*
tooth	*teeth*
vertex	*vertices or vertexes*
woman	*women*

PLURALS – NOUNS WHICH DON'T CHANGE

*Just to confuse you even more, there are some **nouns** which don't change at all when they're pluralised! Here are examples of the most common of these...*

Singular	Plural
aircraft	*aircraft*
deer	*deer*
elk	*elk*
fish	*fish*
hovercraft	*hovercraft*
offspring	*offspring*
moose	*moose*
salmon	*salmon*
series	*series*
sheep	*sheep*
spacecraft	*spacecraft*
species	*species*
trout	*trout*
tuna	*tuna*
watercraft	*watercraft*

RELATIVE PRONOUNS

*A **relative pronoun** is a **pronoun** that's used to refer to **nouns**, altering them or telling us more about them. **Relative pronouns** are also used to introduce a **relative clause**.*

(SEE ALSO RELATIVE CLAUSES BELOW)

The most common relative pronouns are **who, whom, that, where, which, when, whoever, whomever, whose** and **whichever**. Other relative pronouns include **whatever** (meaning *anything that*), **wherever** (meaning *at any place*) and **whenever** (meaning *at any time*).

RELATIVE CLAUSES

*Once you know all your **relative pronouns**, then **relative clauses** are dead easy.*

*A **relative clause** is simply a type of **subordinate clause** that gives extra information about a **noun**, you just connect it to the **main clause** of a sentence using a **relative pronoun**. It can go in the middle of a sentence, using two **commas** to make it an **embedded clause** or you can add it to the end of your **main clause** with a single comma instead. Remember that a **relative clause** usually makes no sense when read on its own...*

Examples of relative clauses

*Cordelia Wilde, **who** was a cryptobiologist, lived at 221d Baker Street, London.*

*It has been estimated that over 100,000 people attended the Coming of Mage ceremony, many of **whom** had known Poppy Copperthwaite since the day she was born.*

*The house **that** the third little pig built was made of bricks.*

*In Codswallop, **where** Alex and Georgie McClellan live, there is a mad and gigantic wild rabbit roaming free.*

*Slipp Manor, **which** had been in the inventor's family for generations, looked in dire and desperate need of repair.*

*Back in 1666, **when** houses were all made of wood, a great fire*

destroyed the city of London.
***Whoever** pulls the sword from the stone shall be declared the true king of England.*
*The prize will go to **whomeve**r is the most successful in completing the task that I've given them.*
*Magda, **whose** eyes were the deepest green, sighed as she remembered all that she'd lost.*
*You may finish your work at break or lunchtime, **whichever** you prefer.*
*I don't care, do **whatever** you want to, it doesn't matter to me.*
***Wherever** I lay my hat, that's my home.*
***Whenever** there was a robbery, you could be sure that either the Wardrobe or Mesmerise would be soon on the crime scene.*

RHETORICAL QUESTIONS

Rhetorical questions are one of my favourite literary devices. They are questions which are posed by the character to themselves - or directly to the reader - in order to create a dramatic effect or to make a point, without expecting an answer...

Examples of rhetorical questions
How did it come to this?
What would they both do now?
Where in the world am I?
What on Earth has caused all of this?
When will I ever see her face again?
Where would you hide were you in my shoes?
Why does it always happen to me?
Does it have to end like this?
So – what would you do were you to find yourself in the same position as me?
Why does it always rain on me?
I suppose you're wondering how I got myself in this fine predicament, aren't you?

RULE OF THREE / POWER OF THREE

*The **Rule of Three** - or **Power of Three** - is a writing technique where you use three **adjectives** or examples for description or to illustrate a point as they appear to be stronger and more memorable than using just the one. Wikipedia suggests that by using the **Rule of Three/Power of Three** 'things...are inherently funnier, more satisfying, or more effective than other numbers of things'.*

*The **Rule of Three/Power of Three** is a literary device I use a lot in my own writing...*

Examples

blood, sweat, and tears
cold, dark and dingy
faith, hope and charity
Father, son and the holy ghost
hook, line and sinker
lock, stock and barrel
lost, alone and helpless
love, hope and devotion
mad, bad and dangerous to know
mind, body and soul
morning, noon and night
ready, willing and able
Reduce – Re-use - Recycle
soft, strong and very long
Snap! Crackle! Pop!
Stop, look and listen.
tall, dark and handsome
this, that and the other
work, rest and play

SAID ALTERNATIVES

*It's so easy just to add an **adverb** to the **verb said** to show how someone is speaking when you're. e.g. "Stop" Wilde **said angrily**. However, it shows greater variety if you use alternative words for **said** just like these examples....*

(SEE ALSO SHOW NOT TELL)

Examples of words you could use when linked with curiosity: asked challenged coaxed enquired hinted investigated puzzled queried questioned quizzed requested wondered

Examples of words you could use when linked with a discussion: concluded considered countered debated noted objected out pondered proposed reasoned rebutted refuted reiterated reported speculated stated surmised testified theorised verified

Examples of words you could use when linked with to humour: bantered chortled chuckled giggled joked joshed quipped sniggered tittered

Examples of words you could use when linked with insults: baited bragged dared goaded insulted jeered jibed lied mimicked mocked needled provoked ribbed ridiculed smirked taunted teased tempted

Examples of words you could use when linked to persuasion: advised appealed asserted assured begged beseeched claimed convinced encouraged implored pleaded probed prodded prompted stressed suggested urged

Examples of words you could use when linked to a response: acknowledged added answered argued clarified commented conceded concurred corrected disagreed disputed explained reassured remarked replied responded stated

Examples of words you could use when linked with uncertainty: cautioned confused dithered doubted faltered guessed hesitated paused wavered

Examples of words you could use when showing how a character is speaking: babbled barked bellowed blustered boomed chattered croaked drawled droned groaned hissed hollered howled jabbered mumbled nattered prattled rambled roared screamed screeched shrilled slurred sneezed stammered stuttered thundered twittered wheezed whispered yapped yelled

Examples of words you could use when linked to anger: argued badgered bickered chastised chided complained cursed demanded denounced exploded fumed growled interrupted ordered raged ranted retaliated retorted scolded scowled seethed snapped snarled sneered swore threatened warned

Examples of words you could use when linked with being disgusted: cringed gagged griped groaned grunted moaned mocked rasped refused sniffed snorted

Examples of words you could use when linked with feelings of embarrassment: admitted confessed spilled spluttered

Examples of words you could use when linked with feelings of fear: fretted moaned panted pleaded quavered shivered shrieked shuddered squeaked squealed trembled whimpered worried

Examples of words you could use linked with regret: apologised forgave gulped mumbled murmured muttered sighed wished

Examples of words you could use when linked with surprise: amazed blurted confounded exclaimed gasped marvelled perplexed sputtered

Examples of words you could use when linked with frustration: exasperated huffed maddened protested whined whinged

Examples of words you could use which are linked to feelings of happiness: beamed cheered complimented congratulated crowed grinned gushed hummed praised sang simpered smiled squealed thanked whooped

Examples of words linked you could use linked with feelings of love: blushed cooed expressed flirted proclaimed promised purred swooned

Examples of words you could use linked with sadness: bawled blubbered consoled cried lamented moaned sniffled sobbed wailed wept

Examples of words you could use linked with tiredness: dazedly groggily lethargically listlessly sleepily sluggishly wearily yawned

Examples of words which are not linked to any one particular emotion: added addressed agreed announced began boasted called coached confided confirmed continued decided declared defended described determined dictated disclosed divulged echoed gloated implied informed insisted instructed lectured maintained motioned mouthed mused nodded notified observed offered pestered pressed promised prompted quoted recalled recited reckoned recounted related reminded repeated requested revealed rhymed spoke swore sympathised teased tested told tried uttered ventured volunteered welcomed vowed

SHOW NOT TELL

*If you really want to upskill your writing though, rather than **telling** your reader what a character **said** or how they said it, take it to the next level and use **show not tell** techniques instead...*

Examples of show - not tell

Telling the reader... *He laughed loudly.*
Showing the reader instead... *Humphry rolled about on the floor, clutching his sides as though stopping them from splitting as he gasped for breath.*
"Oh, that's priceless, Pippy Clutterbuck!" he eventually spluttered, "He got you good and proper there!"

Telling the reader... *She was angry.*
Showing the reader instead... *A red mist descended over Cordelia's eyes as she stared at the man stood before her. She could feel her fingers ball into fists as the rage which now possessed her threatened to erupt into violence.*

Telling the reader... *Nona cried at the news of her grandfather's death.*
Showing the reader instead... *Nona sank to her knees as the tears streamed down her face. How could the man who she loved more than anyone else no longer be there? What would become of her now?*

Telling the reader... *Mason was frightened*
Showing the reader instead... *The young reporter could feel a lump in his throat as though the fear Mason now felt was choking him as he stared at the huge and hideous creature which was now deliberately making its way towards him.*
"Please," Mason heard his feeble voice plead, "spare me..."

Telling the reader... *The house was old and abandoned.*
Showing the reader instead... *They could hear their footsteps*

echo on the time-worn wooden stairs, as bare and naked as the day they'd first been built. Each step moaned at the weight being placed on them, it being so long since someone – anyone – had entered the quiet solitude of the ghost of what was once a home.

Telling the reader... *The walls were plain and empty.*
Showing the reader instead... *On the walls were the silhouettes of the pictures which had once hung there, the wallpaper having peeled from where it met the ceiling, the dried water-stains showing where the roof had failed to prevent the rain from entering the building.*

Telling the reader... *The night was frosty and cold..*
Showing the reader instead... *Alex could see his breath curl before him, like snakes of smoke, as he waited for Georgie to return. He rubbed his hands together, desperately trying to get his blood circulating again as the chill of the night bit deeply into them...*

Telling the reader... *Zac could smell smoke.*
Showing the reader instead... *Zac almost gagged at the acrid stench that now filled his nostrils. He could feel his eyes begin to water and sting as he coughed violently, Zac's chest fitfully heaving as it frantically sought the oxygen it so desperately needed.*

SEMI-COLONS

*A **semi-colon** (;) is a type of **punctuation** either used to make lists already containing commas easier to understand or to separate two closely related but **main** or **independent clauses** - complete thoughts – both of which could then stand alone as sentences of their own.*

*However, **semi-colons** are also one of the most commonly misused pieces of **punctuation**. Always remember that **semi-colons** shouldn't be used to connect more than two **clauses**. You also shouldn't capitalise the first word of the second **clause** after a **semi-colon** as per the examples below....*

Examples of lists with semi-colons:

Juliette's travels took her to: Baker Street, London; The Needles, Isle of Wight and Dartmoor, Devon.

You will need: a pen, paper and ruler; a water bottle and a reading book.

Examples of sentences with semi-colons:

Humphry had already polished off a huge breakfast; however, he was already hungry again.

I felt the hands of dread choking me, leaving me to silently scream for help; but then the voice of reason gently replied, soothing me, reassuring me...

Cordelia hadn't seen the other airship rapidly approaching until it was much too late; now there was a huge rip in the side of the Icarus.

The remote control needs new batteries; otherwise, we'll not be able to travel back in time again.

There is growing evidence that Prime Minister Norris Rongen is covering things up; of course, most people will never believe it of him though.

Earlier that year, Sherwood had moved to Scallywag Bay; he preferred the tranquility of the countryside over the hustle and bustle of London.

SETTING DESCRIPTIONS

*When writing narratives, it is important that you set the scene for your readers when describing **settings** and **locations**. Here are some words and phrases for you to help paint a picture for them...*

Examples of words and phrases showing what you can see there: birds soaring, boats bobbing, blistered bannisters, brilliant lights, children playing, crashing waves breaking on the shoreline, darkening skies, darkness falling, dawn breaking, decaying buildings, deserted rooms, dilapidated rooftops, fields of gold, ghostly spiderwebs, grimy window panes, lifeless forms, lush green meadows, murky waters, people waiting, peeling wallpaper, rusty railings, shadowy figures, shattered glass windows, silhouetted outlines, sinister shapes, skeletal figures, spectral lights, splintered/stained floorboards, sun rising/setting, twisted branches, sweeping beaches, unkempt gardens, water-stained ceilings, weathered wood, rippling curtains, trains thundering past, trees swaying

Examples of words and phrases showing what you hear there: agonising shrieks, anguished howls, banging doors, bats echoing, birds squawking, blood-curdling cries, crashing waves, creaking hinges, chanting voices, deafening silence, ear-splitting screams, moaning cries, floorboards creaking, haunting noises, heated discussions, hushed tones, muffled muttering, muted voices, pitter-patter of raindrops, rattling windows, strangled screams, scuffling footsteps, shouting, shuffling feet, sirens wailing, tapping fingers, ticking clocks, thudding footsteps, traffic roaring past, tormented whispering, wind whistling

Examples of words and showing what you smell there: acrid, bitter, decay, disgusting, foul, gut-churning, horrifying, intoxicating, mouldy, musty, nauseating, offensive, pungent, putrid, rancid, repulsive, revolting, rot, rotten, sickening, sick-inducing, stale, stomach-wrenching, suffocating, unfamiliar, vile

Examples of words and phrases showing how you sense things there: alienness, ambition, being watched, desperation, despair, emptiness, eeriness, evil presence, foreboding, impending doom, hopelessness, hunger, longing, malevolence, menace numbness, nerve-tingling, ominous, suspicion, threatening, uncomfortable, uneasiness, unpleasant, unsettling, unwelcoming, wrong

Examples of words showing what the weather is like there: airy arctic biting bitter blanketed blazing blowy blustery bright brisk chilling cloudless cloudy crisp damp dank darkened dewy dismal downpours drab drafty drizzly dull dusky foggy foul freezing fresh frosty glacial gloomy grey gusty howling icy misty murky overcast piercing pleasant plentiful pounding pouring radiant raging rain raindrops raw roaring sharp showery soggy sparkling summery sunless sweltering tempestuous thundery torrential rain trickling turbulent violent wet wild windy windswept wintry

Examples of words showing how you feel there: afraid alone angry anxious apprehensive bitter bored. breathing butterflies cheerful comfortable concerned confident confused depressed desperate despondent distressed downhearted eager ecstatic emotional enthusiastic fearful fed-up frantic frightened frowning frustrated gloomy goosebumps happy heart-broken hopeless horrified insecure irritated isolated lonely malicious miserable nervous overawed overwhelmed pained petrified pleased pressured proud refreshed relaxed relieved reluctant scared settled shocked solemn stressed surprised tense terrified thoughtful trembling uneasy upset violent wide-eyed worried

SIMILES

Similes are a way of describing something by comparing it to something else using the words **like** or **as**. Many **similes** are already familiar sayings such as **bright as a button**, or **as quiet as a mouse**. Here are a few more examples for you to use, borrow or adapt...

as silent as a graveyard
as cold as ice
like the back of my hand
as black as night
as blind as a bat
as brave as a lion
as bright as a button
as clean as a whistle
as clear as mud
as cold as ice
as common as muck
as cunning as a fox
as dead as a doornail
as deaf as a post
as deep as the ocean
as dry as a bone
as dull as watching paint dry
as easy as abc
as fast as a cheetah
as fit as a fiddle
as flat as a pancake
as free as a bird
as fresh as a daisy
as gentle as a lamb
as good as gold
as graceful as a swan
as hard as nails
as helpless as a baby

as honest as the day is long
as light as a feather
as old as the hills
as pale as a ghost
as sharp as a knife
as sick as a dog
as slippery as a snake
as smooth as a baby's bottom
as solid as a rock
as stiff as a board
as straight as an arrow
as sweet as sugar
as thin as a rake
as tough as leather
climbs like a monkey
eyes like a hawk
fight like cats and dogs
fit as a fiddle
fit like a glove
floats like a butterfly
howled like a hungry wolf
like leaves on a blustery day
rain falls like teardrops
runs like the wind
slept like a baby
soared like an eagle.
stings like a bee
as white as pearls

SENTENCE OPENERS - TIME

Making a welcome return to our book are more adverbials - this time with time examples you can use or change ...
(SEE ALSO ADVERBIALS AND FRONTED ADVERBIALS)

A moment later, life as he knew it had changed forever...
A short while later, all was calm once again...
After a while, quiet had filled the room and order restored...
After that she knew her only course of action was to escape...
After what seemed an eternity, they arrived at their destination...
Afterwards, they wondered if it had all been worth the effort...
All of a sudden, the door was flung opened and there stood...
As soon as she saw him, she knew that everything would be all right...
At last, they were home, safe in the knowledge that...
Before too long, the train slowly pulled into the station...
During the time it took them to reach there...
In the meantime, the others had begun to abandon all hope...
Later on that evening, he looked back on the events that day...
Long ago, when the moon was still new to the night sky...
Meanwhile, unbeknown to them, other events were unfolding not too far away from them...
Next week will be different, he thought to himself.
Now it was the moment they'd all been waiting for...
Once, when the world was over two thousand years old...
One day, a day not much different to any other one...
One evening that all changed and not for the better either...
One morning, as the sun peeked its face over the horizon...
Soon it would be time to put right all that was wrong...

SENTENCE OPENERS – ORDER

Additional openers to help when writing in chronological order.
*e.g. **Firstly, Secondly, Thirdly, Lastly** etc.*

At first, they thought that they were the only ones there.
After what seemed an eternity, the door slowly opened.
First came the Vikings, followed by the Saxons.
Second to arrive that evening was the scowling Fenella Gogglewick.
Then it was Doyley's turn to speak to the police.
Next, take the metal out and see if it has turned to gold.
Last but by no means least, came the familiar figure of Gil.
Finally, the coast was clear so Magda made her escape.

SENTENCE OPENERS - PLACE

*More openers using **prepositions**, with examples for you to use...*
(SEE ALSO PREPOSITIONAL PHRASES)

At the end of the tunnel, they could see a blinding light.
Beside the rail track they found the body...
Far away from all they'd left behind they found happiness...
In a far-off land where light and dark battle one another...
In the distance she could see land on the horizon...
In the middle of the night, they silently came for him...
Inside the castle, fly-filled cobwebs hung in every corner...
Nearby, a nightingale sang as though saying all was well...
Next to the mantelpiece stood an old grandfather clock...
On top of the hill stood a solitary house, much different to the others...
Opposite the house was a police station, but nothing was ever safe in Chapel Street...
Over the bridge they ran, desperate to reach safety...
Under the bridge the troll waited silently and patiently, hoping to hear the clip-clip of hooves above his ugly head...

SENTENCE OPENERS – COMPARISONS

More examples for you to borrow or adapt when writing sentences which make comparisons in your writing...

(SEE ALSO CONJUNCTIONS)

Although lacking in experience, the young Harryhausen soon made a lasting impression on all those he met.
Despite her young and tender years, Wilde had quickly gained the trust of those around her
Even though the odds were initially against them, they still won out in the end.
However difficult the task seemed at first glance, Slipp had eventually managed to solve the problem he'd been set.
Rather than accepting that their plight was hopeless, Miss Morgan was determined to prove everyone wrong once again.
Still, there are many questions to be asked about that night.
Unlike those she'd started term with at the Valiant with, Jude had no parents to go home to every weekend.
Yet sometimes, when you might least expect it, you will still hear his pitiful cries for help long into the night.

SENTENCE OPENERS – ADDITIONAL INFORMATION

Make your writing even more interesting by adding extra detail...

Again, Wilde chose to ignore her friends' advice and went anyway.
Along with fame and fortune comes the lack of privacy.
Also, make sure to turn the lights off before going to bed.
Another thing to consider is how difficult it may be to achieve.
As well as making you fitter, exercise is good for your mental health too.
For example, the word flush can be a noun, verb or adjective!

SENTENCE OPENERS – INTRODUCTIONS

*Here are some starters to help when you **debate, discuss, persuade** or **inform**...*

(SEE ALSO PERSUASIVE WORDS)

A popular opinion is.... After discovering... Are you aware that...
As a result of... As recent studies show... At the moment...
Certainly, Clearly, Current dat indicates...
Current research suggests... Despite the fact that...
Evidence suggest that... Following recent event...
For these reasons... Furthermore...
From the moment you first hear/see/meet...
Imagine if... In previous years...
In support of this... In the past few weeks/months/years...
It has been reported that... It has been said that...
It is almost certain that... It is certain that...
It is thought that... It is vital that...
It is vitally important that... Nevertheless,
Latest research implies... Many people believe...
Opinion polls show... Meanwhile, Moreover,
Most people assume...
Most people are of the opinion... Most people assume...
Similarly, Nevertheless,
No one can deny that...
One of the main arguments is that...
Opinion polls show... Recent events suggest that... Recently,
Regarding recent events... Research shows... Similarly,
Statistics show... Surely, This argument aims to...
Unbelievably,
Within the opinion piece...
Within this balanced argument...
Within this report...
Without a doubt,

SENTENCE OPENERS – CONCLUSIONS

*Made your point? Time to conclude your **debate, discussion, information text** or **persuasive piece** using a sentence starter below...*
(SEE ALSO PERSUASIVE WORDS)

Accordingly... After carefully consideration...
After considering all the facts...
After considering all the information available...
After studying both viewpoints/opinions etc.
As a consequence... As a result...
As recent studies have shown... As stated in my introduction...
As you can see... By comparison... Consequently,
Conversely. Despite the evidence... Finally,
For these reasons... From now on... Generally,
Given all the points mentioned...
Having taken all the evidence into account...
Having taken everything into consideration...
I strongly believe... In addition to this, In comparison,
In conclusion... In fact... In my opinion, In summary...
It is an undeniable truth that... It is important to remember ...
It is obvious that... It seems as though... Just imagine...
Lastly... Obviously, On the other hand... Overall...
Subsequently... Surely... Therefore, I conclude...
Therefore, I strongly believe...
Therefore, it is my opinion...
Therefore, my view is...
Therefore, to sum up...
Therefore...
This is evidenced by... This is proven by...
To conclude... To summarise...
Ultimately... Unbelievably... Undoubtedly...
Weighing everything up... Without doubt,

SUPER STORY STARTS

For me, the most important part of a story is its beginning.
How a story starts can often be the make-or-break moment for any reader, so it's important to instantly make a connection and draw them in within a page or two so that they want to read more.
There' no right way to start a story only wrong ones where the reader soon puts down the book without going any further.
Here are a few suggestions - with examples - of the type of super story starts you might use when you next write one of your own...

Super Story Start I – *Hook 'em in!*

One of the best ways to draw the reader in at the start of your story is to create a *hook* – something that will generate intrigue and get them wondering what will happen next. Starting your story this way helps to keep the reader guessing and encourages them to read on...

It's on nights like these that my mind wanders back to those last few years of primary school. Naturally, my thoughts turn to Billy Pepper and I often wonder – did they ever find him?

Super Story Start II – *And...action!*

Starting with some action immediately helps to create a sense of excitement in the reader but can be dangerous as you might then leave yourself nowhere else to go if it's not done effectively.
Remember – your action sequence should lead into the story without overshadowing any showdowns or the eventual ending.

Sophie crouched low in the shadows, watching as the searchlights swept the area around her. She felt the veins pound against her temples, the sound of her heart drumming in her ears as she peered at the door ahead of her.
It's now or never, she thought to herself as she sprung from her hiding place and made her final, desperate bid for freedom.

Super Story Start III – *Using speech or dialogue.*
When done well, speech or dialogue at the beginning of your story - without explanation – can entice your reader to want to discover the story behind it. However, be sure not to confuse the reader, especially if it's the first time they've come across your characters or the events you're writing about...

"Ellis, you're going to miss the bus if you don't get a move on!" his mum screamed again, his stepsiblings joining in, sounding like cats calling for their dinner.
"I'm on the loo!"
"Still?"
"Yes!" Ellis shouted.
In truth, he wasn't actually doing anything, just sitting there, sapped of the energy or desire to move off it.
"One of these days you're going to flush yourself away, the amount of time you spend on that thing in the morning," his mum shouted unsympathetically.
"If only I could..." Ellis muttered, reaching for the toilet roll with one hand as he flushed the toilet with the other, without even bothering to get off the seat.
That's when it happened...

Super Story Start IV – *Question Time.*
Asking questions as a starter is another good way to open your story as you are instantly engaging with the reader, causing then to wonder both the answer to your question and where your story might eventually lead them. Starting this way leaves the reader with no other choice but to read on to find out more...

Have you ever been caught up in an argument between two other people? You know, when there are the three of you who are either friends or relatives and two of them disagree about something or other.
Or they have an inexplicable falling out over something stupid

or trivial and you're the one caught right slap-bang in the middle of it?
In my experience, it can usually go one of three ways - you pick sides, refuse to choose between them or somehow you find that you are no longer part of a trio anymore...

Super Story Start V – *Tales of the Unexpected...*

An unexpected start can immediately create a sense of mystery, urgency and suspense. Beginning your story this way can instantly put the reader on the back foot, causing them to wonder how on Earth your character got to that point in their lives. Using an unexpected starter can make your reader more committed to reading your story to the end...

This is it...
The end...
My final curtain...
All alone, save those who are now waiting around, ready to flick the switch, signalling the end of me.
How did it come to this?
Why did it have to come to this?
Now, in my final moments, my whole past is playing out before me, reminding me of when I was popular, wanted and loved, rather than lost, abandoned and deserted.
Where are those who I helped forget their problems when they needed me too?
Where are those I made laugh and cry for countless hours on end?
Where are those who came to me when they wanted to escape from their everyday, humdrum lives?
Nowhere to be seen.
Yet again...

Super Story Start VI – *A little bit of background to begin with.*

Sharing some extra background information on a character or

characters they may come across is another way to engage your reader as soon as they read the first few lines of your story...

We'd only lived on Pine Grove for a matter of days before I first came across Leo Tomasi. He was exactly the same age as me, even sharing the same birthday, but almost twice the size and weight. However, I immediately knew from the moment I met him that we'd be BFFs and so that's proven to be the case for the past eleven years.

Super Story Start VII – *Setting the scene.*
Another effective way of captivating your reader is introducing your setting straight away so that they can imagine being there, side by side with the character...

Amir had always loved the treehouse, nestled as it was high in the gnarled branches of the old sycamore tree which stood alone in the back of his yard. When he was in it, Amir felt like he was the king of the world as he gazed out across the fields that stretched as far as the eye could see, the carpet of green only ending where it met the river which ran the length of the horizon.

Super Story Start VIII – *Let me introduce myself...*
Rather than taking all the time and effort to introduce your characters or set the scene, why not instead have them introduce himself/herself/themselves to your readers in either an interesting, surprising or an unusual way...

Hi, I'm Albie and I'm 11 years old. I like playing football, rugby and tennis – but not at the same time!
Now, what else can I tell you about myself...? Oh, that's right - I almost forget...
I help the undead.

Super Story Start IX – *A shock to the system.*

Writing an opening which has a strong element of danger to it can shock or startle your reader into wanting to continue to read on. They will instantly want to know who your character is, where they are and what is happening to them, as well as whether they manage to make to the end of the story...

As she stared down at the stormy waves which crashed against the jagged rocks that littered the shoreline below, Courtney Ferguson wondered who would find her body after she was gone...

Super Story Start X – *Short and snappy.*

A short and snappy start, using sentences or speech with only one or two words, can also grab a reader's attention, creating an immediate sense of fear or tension. These story starters can automatically create a sense of danger, intrigue or mystery...

"Quick – hide!"

Super Story Start XI– *Strangely unusual..*

Strange or unusual starters are an effective way of showing any reader there's something different about your story. Immediately, it captures their attention as they begin to puzzle over the meaning of your opening, almost demanding that they continue to read your story to discover what it's all about...

Although it was a potentially explosive situation, nobody ever expected Curtis to do just that – explode...

Super Story Start XII – *To prologue or not to prologue...?*

If written well, a prologue can often create a sense of suspense to hold the attention of those reading it.
However, you also run the risk that the reader may not want to know the events which have happened before so you need

to make your prologues both exciting and purposeful so that they will continue to read on...

Faster he ran, the rain driving against his face as he staggered through the trees.
Behind him he could hear the cries of his pursuers, calling to one another, seeking him out, coordinating their search for him. He knew the net was drawing tighter around him, but his natural instincts were still strong. He had to escape and warn the others otherwise his efforts would have amounted to nothing and the past few months would have all been in vain.

Super Story Start XIII – *Oh, what an atmosphere...*

Readers can't resist an atmospheric opening, especially when discovering that something terrible has happened or you are about to embark on a great adventure with them.

It's like they're there in that moment, sharing or living the experience themselves, often leaving them with more questions than answers...

Such a shame really.
So young, yet so willing, though to be fair to the girl, she had put up quite a struggle once she realised what was going to happen to her when she realised what kind of creature I was.
No doubt it made the kill more invigorating, removing the guilt from feeding on a school friend, though really she was in truth more of acquaintance actually...

Super Story Start XIV – *Baffle, bemuse and confuse them...*

Want to really get your readers thinking? Then write a story start which will baffle, bemuse and confuse. Do it well and they will keep returning to the beginning to check their understanding as the story continues...

It was the last day of never and we were all ready to go home...

Super Story Start XV – *It's a mystery, oh it's a mystery...*
What better way could there be to begin a story than a riddle, a puzzle or a mystery to solve?
An opening which teases the reader with a question or an unsolved clue means that they then spend the rest of the story trying to find the answer to it.
This is a really good way to start your story, especially if it is a classic whodunnit or a *Scooby-Doo* type mystery where the villain is revealed at the end...

Those who were there that evening swore that when Lady Merrywinter turned in for the night, she was in the rudest of health and was positive about the future.
However, when her maid entered her room the following morning to serve Lady Merrywinter her breakfast, the widow's mood and appearance had somehow changed. Some say that she was an entirely different woman altogether...
But it would take those of us who were there several weeks to work out what had really happened to the kindly old lady we knew and loved, as well as discovering who the imposter who replaced her actually was...

Super Story Start XVI – *Flash Forwards...*
By starting your story with a time jump, your readers will immediately want to know what has happened to your character/characters and the events which have already led them to that point in their story.
However, this type of story starter requires you to then revisit it at some point so that your tale is then fully complete...

The celebrations marking thirty years since the end of World War IV had hardly begun before First Prophet Suu Kyi Htun slipped away from them, unseen and unnoticed by her adoring public.
Now, as she sat alone in what was once the presidential office

before the Great Cleansing, Suu Kyi stared at the videographic she held in her hand, smiling sadly as her dead sister waved back at her.
"You shouldn't have done it, Suu Lai," she whispered as her mind drifted back to the day when the Htun twins changed the world as we once knew it forever...

Super Story Start XVII – *Flashback...*
It stands to reason that if you start a story by flashing forwards, then a good old-fashioned flashback is another good way to draw your reader in.
A flashback could be a memory, a dream or simply someone retelling the events of long ago...

"Tell us a story, Dad."
"Yes please, Daddy!"
I smiled as I looked into the expectant faces of my two children.
"All right," I said, patting either side of me as they bounced onto the sofa, wrapping themselves into my arms, "What story would you like to hear?"
But I knew which one it would be as soon as the question had left my lips.
"The one about you and Auntie Ceri during the war," my daughter Maddie smiled.

Super Story Start XVIII – *Read all about it!*
Last but by no means least in my super story starts is the newspaper report. This is a particular favourite story starter method of mine as it can be a really effective way to start a story and can be used as a flashback, a prologue or simply by setting the scene. By using a newspaper report, you can quickly fill in the blanks for the reader whilst tempting them to find out more about the events being reported at the start of your story. This saves you having to write pages and pages to provide additional background information important to your plot ...

SATANIC SCHOOL SCANDAL
Super-Headteacher Suspected of Foul Play
St. Godrics Telegraph 10^h August
by Jonas Lane

Mystery surrounds the arrest on Tuesday night of a well-respected and influential member of the local education authority.
Elrond Hubbard, 55, of Church Lane, St Godrics was discovered in the grounds of George Orwell School at around midnight last night by two police constables who were conducting their nightly patrol of the area.

I hope that the suggestions and the few examples I've given help to inspire you when writing you own story starters.

There are literally hundreds of ways for you to introduce your tale, the choice of how to start them being entirely yours.

However, the most important thing for all young writers to remember when starting a story is to find a way to instantly grab the reader's attention so that they stay with it from the very first word read to the very last...

SUFFIXES – GENERAL RULES

*Suffixes are a string of letters which go at the end of a **root word**, changing or adding to its meaning. They show if a word is a **noun**, an **adjective**, an **adverb** or a **verb**.*

*Adding **suffixes** to root **words** can be tricky to remember, but learning the following well-known **suffix** rules will help you choose how and when to use them correctly.*

However, you also need to remember that there are again exceptions to every suffix rule...

(SEE ALSO SPELLINGS)

The first thing to know is that there are two kinds of suffixes - **consonant suffixes** which begin with a **consonant** (*-s, -ful, -less, - ness, -ly, ment etc.*) and **vowel suffixes** (*a, e, i, o, u*) which - as you've already guessed - begin with a **vowel** (*-ing, -ed, -er, -es, -end -est, -y etc.*).

When adding a **consonant suffix**, you normally just need to add the **consonant suffix** to the end of your **root word**.

Examples
abandon + ***ment suffix*** becomes *abandonment*
hope + ***ful suffix*** becomes *hopeful*
love + ***ly suffix*** becomes *lovely*
quiet + ***ness suffix*** becomes *quietness*
rest + ***less suffix*** becomes *restless*
shoe + ***s suffix*** becomes *shoes*

Of course, there are exceptions to this rule - especially if the
root word ends with the ***letter i.***
(SEE SUFFIX RULE 5 THAT FOLLOWS)

However, when adding a ***vowel suffix***, you must always check how the ***root word*** is spelt first and then – generally - apply one of the following ***suffix*** rules...

Suffix rule 1 - Double the consonant.
Sometimes adding suffixes to root words which end with a *consonant* requires you to double the last letter...

- *Root words* with a *short vowel* and *one consonant at the end*

If a *root word* ends with a *short vowel* sound followed by a *single consonant*, the last letter of the *root word* will need to be doubled before you add the *suffix* to it.

Examples
chop + *-ed suffix* becomes *chopped*
hot + *-er suffix* becomes *hotter*
run + *-ing suffix* becomes *running*
skip + *-ed suffix* becomes *skipped*
sun + *-y suffix* becomes *sunny*

- *Root words* with *more than one syllable* and the *letter l* at the end

If a *root word* has more than *one syllable* and *ends with the letter l*, you then need to *double the letter l* when adding the *suffix* to it.

Examples
expel + *-ed suffix* becomes *expelled*
fulfill + *-ing suffix* becomes *fulfilling*
patrol + *-ed suffix* become *patrolled*

Exceptions to the double the consonant rule
Please note that the doubling rule does not apply to words which end with the letters *w, x* or *y.*

Suffix rule 2 – Dropping the *silent letter e*.
Dropping the final **silent letter e** from your **root word** depends

on whether the first letter of the **suffix** you are adding is either a **vowel** or **consonant**.

- If adding a *vowel suffix* to a *root word* that ends with a *silent letter e*

If your *root word* ends with the *silent letter e* and you are adding a *vowel suffix*, then drop the final *e* from your *root word* before adding the *suffix* to it.

Examples
bake + *-er suffix* becomes *baker*
dispose + *-able suffix* becomes *disposable*
sense *+ible suffix* becomes *sensible*
share + *-ing suffix* becomes *sharing*

Exceptions to the *silent letter e* rule
Just to help confuse matters, there are some *root words* where you would think that you would drop the *silent letter e* when you add the *vowel suffix*, but – guess what? – the *silent letter e* has to be kept when you add the *suffix!*

Examples
change + *-able suffix* becomes *changeable*
love + *-able suffix* becomes *loveable*
replace + *-able suffix* becomes *replaceable*

Suffix rule 3 - Keeping the *final letter e* at the end of the *root word*.
There are other occasions when the *final letter e* should be kept in place at the end of your *root word* after you add a *suffix*...

- *Root words* ending with either *ce* or *ge*

If the *root word* ends with the letters *ce* or *ge* and the *suffix* begins with either *a* or *o*, the *final letter e* should stay in place at the end of the *root word*.

Examples
courage + *-ous suffix* becomes *courageous*
exchange + *-able suffix* becomes *exchangeable*
notice + *-able suffix* become *noticeable*

- *Root words* ending with either *ee* or *ye*

This rule also applies if your *root word* ends with *ee* or *ye*, you keep the *final letter e* at the end of your *root word* before adding your *suffix* to it.

Examples
agree + *-ing suffix* becomes *agreeing*
eye + *-ing suffix* becomes *eyeing*
see + *-ing suffix* becomes *seeing*

You'll also need to remember to keep the *final letter e* if you're adding the *suffix -ly*.

Examples
definite + *-ly suffix* becomes *definitely*
late + *-ly suffix* becomes *lately*
love + *-ly suffix* becomes *lovely*

- Keep the *final letter e* when adding the *consonant suffix –ful*

Again, you keep the *e* when you add the *consonant suffix -ful* to *root words* which end with the *final letter e*.

Examples
grace + *-ful suffix* becomes *graceful*
hope + *-ful suffix* becomes *hopeful*
spite + *-ful suffix* becomes *spiteful*

Suffix rule 4 - Keeping the *final letter y* at the end of your root word.

As well as the *final letter e*, there are also many occasions when you will need to keep the *final letter y* at the end of your *root word* when you add your *suffix*.

- *Root words* that end with a *vowel* then the *letter y*

If your *root word* ends with the *letter y* but has a *vowel* directly before it, then keep the *y* at the end of your *root word* before adding your *suffix*.

Examples
betray + *-ed suffix* becomes *betrayed*
buy + *-ing suffix* becomes *buying*
play + *-ful suffix* becomes *playful*

- Adding a *suffix* starting with the **letter** *i* to a *root word* that ends with the *letter y*

If you are adding a *vowel suffix* that begins with the *letter i*, then you keep the *letter y* at the end of your *root word*.

Examples
copy + *-ing suffix* becomes *copying*
carry + *-ing suffix* becomes *marrying*
hurry + *-ing suffix* becomes *hurrying*

Remember that a word shouldn't have two *letter i's* in a row — however there is the odd exception of course...

ski + *ing suffix* becomes *skiing*!

Suffix rule 5 – When to change the *final letter y* to the letter *i* before adding a *suffix*.

Often, there will be times when you will need to change the *final letter y* at the end of your *root word* and replace it with the *letter i* before you can add your *suffix* to it.

- For *root words* which end with a *consonant* then the *letter y*

If the *root word* has a *consonant* before the *letter y* at the end, you will need to change the *letter y* to the *letter i* before adding your suffix.

Examples
angry + *ier suffix* becomes *angrier*
greedy + *ly suffix* becomes *greedily*
lonely + *-ness suffix* becomes *loneliness*

Exceptions to changing the letter y to the letter i rule.
Not surprisingly, there are some exceptions to this particular rule...

Examples
fry + *-er suffix* becomes *fryer*
enjoy + *-ment suffix* becomes *enjoyment*

Suffix Rule 6 - *Root words* ending *ie* - change the *letters ie* to the *letter y* before adding your *suffix*.

If your root ends with the *letters ie*, you change them to the *letter y* before you add the *vowel suffix -ing*.

Examples
die + *-ing suffix* becomes *dying*
lie + *-ing suffix* becomes *lying*
untie + *-ing suffix* becomes *untying*

Got all that? Probably not as it used to confuse me too when I was your age! So, to help you remember, here's a list of all the suffixes, along with some examples, you are supposed to know before you go to secondary school – as well as a few others you might need when writing.

You can also find more examples of these in the **SPELLINGS** section of this book...

SUFFIXES – GENERAL LIST AND MEANINGS

*Some of the **suffixes** below belong to each other whilst others use hyphens.*

(SEE ALSO PLURALS, SPELLINGS and HYPHENS)

Suffix	Meaning	Example(s)
-able	*can be done*	comfortable
-acy	*state or quality*	privacy democracy
-age	*result of an action*	marriage pilgrimage
-al	*relating to*	personal legal
-ance	*state or quality of*	dominance
-ant	*having an effect*	disinfectant
-ant	*condition or state*	brilliant pregnant
-ant	*thing or a being*	mutant
-ary	*place or collection of*	glossary library
-ary	*one who*	secretary
-ate	*become*	demonstrate hesitate
-ative	*having the nature of*	creative imaginative
-ation	*act or process*	creation information
-based	*playing a major part of*	computer-based,
-cian	*one who is/does*	optician magician
-cy	*state or quality*	urgency fluency
-ed	*past-tense verbs*	turned cooked
-ee	*one who is/does*	employee amputee
-eer	*one who is/does*	pioneer engineer
-en	*made of*	wooden golden
-en	*being made*	broaden lighten

Suffix	Meaning	Example(s)
-ence	*state or quality of*	coincidence
-eous	*having the nature of*	gaseous gorgeous
-er	*more/less comparative*	higher sooner
-er	*one who is/does*	painter singer
-er	*that which does*	dishwasher toaster
-es	*more than one of*	boxes dresses
-est	*more/less superlative*	greatest smallest
-free	*without*	carefree pain-free
-ful	*full of*	careful forgetful
-fy	*become or make*	defy
-graph	*to write*	autograph telegraph
-hood	*condition or state*	childhood motherhood
-ial	*relating to*	partial facial
-ible	*can be done*	responsible possible
-ic	*relating to*	heroic historic
-ics	*the study of*	genetics electronics
-ied	*past-tense verbs*	tidied worried
-ier	*more/less comparative*	grumpier wealthier
-ier	*one who is/does*	glazier cashier
-ies	*more than one of*	babies stories
-iest	*more/less superlative*	happiest cheekiest
-ify	*cause to be in/become*	clarify magnify
-ing	*action or process*	eating dancing
-ion	*act or process*	occasion
-ious	*full of*	ambitious religious
-ise	*cause to be or become*	apologise modernise
-ish	*sort of/approximately*	childish foolish
-ism	*belief or behaviour*	feminism heroism
-ist	*one who is/does*	optimist pianist
-ian	*one who is/does*	librarian comedian
-ity	*a state of*	infinity sanity
-ive	*having the nature of*	passive aggressive
-itive	*adjective form of noun*	fugitive positive
-less	*without*	careless fearless

Suffix	Meaning	Example(s)
-like	*resemble another*	alike child-like
-ly	*characteristic of*	quickly roughly
-ment	*action or process*	enjoyment fulfilment
-ness	*state or quality of*	happiness kindness
-ocracy	*form of government*	autocracy democracy
-ocrat	*ruling person*	autocrat democrat
-ology	*the study or science of*	archaeology biology
-ological	*the study or science of*	biological geological
-or	*someone/thing who*	editor inspector
-ous	*full of*	famous jealous
-port	*to carry*	report transport
-proof	*protecting against/safe*	waterproof
-sion	*the condition/state of*	collusion conclusion
-ssion	*the result of*	permission possession
-ship	*art, skill or condition of*	friendship leadership
-tion	*process or act*	attraction projection
-tive	*tending to...*	creative positive
-ty	*state of*	amnesty poverty
-s	*more than one*	books trees shoes
-y	*characterised by*	funny happy sunny

SYNONYMS

*Synonyms are words which means the same as - or is similar to - another word which doesn't have to be an **adjective**. You can find **synonyms** to any word you want by using a **thesaurus** but in the meantime, here are a hundred or so to help get you started...*

Word	Synonyms		
amazing	*incredible*	*astounding*	*improbable*
anger	*enrage*	*infuriate*	*incensed*
angry	*fuming*	*furious*	*enraged*
answer	*reply*	*respond*	*riposte*
ask	*question*	*query*	*interrogate*
awful	*horrible*	*terrible*	*unpleasant*
bad	*wicked*	*rotten*	*sinful*
beautiful	*gorgeous*	*impressive*	*magnificent*
begin	*start*	*open*	*commence*
big	*enormous*	*massive*	*gigantic*
brave	*courageous*	*fearless*	*intrepid*
break	*ruin*	*crash*	*demolish*
bright	*glittering*	*radiant*	*vivid*
calm	*quiet*	*peaceful*	*serene*
come	*reach*	*approach*	*arrive*
cool	*icy*	*cold*	*frosty*
crooked	*bent*	*twisted*	*warped*
cry	*weep*	*moan*	*sob*
cut	*slice*	*carve*	*tear*
dangerous	*hazardous*	*treacherous*	*risky*
dark	*sinister*	*murky*	*shadowy*
decide	*determine*	*choose*	*agree*
definite	*certain*	*sure*	*positive*
delicious	*tasty*	*delectable*	*luscious*
describe	*portray*	*illustrate*	*picture*
destroy	*abolish*	*demolish*	*ruin*
difference	*disagreement*	*variety*	*contrast*
do	*execute*	*organise*	*ensure*

Word	Synonyms		
dull	lifeless	gloomy	tiresome
eager	keen	enthusiastic	passionate
end	stop	finish	dismiss
enjoy	appreciate	value	relish
explain	elaborate	clarify	define
fair	impartial	unbiased	balance
fall	drop	plunge	topple
false	fake	untrue	bogus
fast	rapid	hasty	swiftly
fat	stout	chubby	plump
fear	anxiety	fear	terror
fly	soar	hover	glide
funny	humorous	amusing	witty
get	acquire	obtain	fetch
go	depart	disappear	leave
good	brilliant	excellent	fantastic
great	remarkable	worthy	extraordinary
happy	pleased	satisfied	delighted
hate	despise	detest	loathe
have	gain	possess	believe
help	aid	assist	encourage
hide	conceal	camouflage	cover
hurry	hasten	urge	rush
hurt	damage	distress	upset
idea	thought	clue	belief
important	necessary	essential	critical
interesting	fascinating	exciting	intelligent
keep	hold	maintain	retain
kill	assassinate	execute	murder
lazy	lethargic	idle	sluggish
little	small	puny	minute
look	observe	inspect	study
love	like	desire	fancy
make	fabricate	manufacture	create

Word		Synonyms	
mark	*impress*	*brand*	*stamp*
mischievous	*naughty*	*roguish*	*impish*
move	*change*	*creep*	*crawl*
neat	*tidy*	*trim*	*smart*
new	*current*	*modern*	*recent*
old	*aged*	*used*	*ancient*
part	*fragment*	*fraction*	*piece*
put	*place*	*assign*	*allocate*
quiet	*serene*	*peaceful*	*restful*
right	*correct*	*accurate*	*truthful*
run	*sprint*	*dash*	*rush*
scared	*terrified*	*fearful*	*petrified*
show	*display*	*exhibit*	*reveal*
slow	*unhurried*	*tedious*	*ponderous*
stop	*halt*	*pause*	*hiatus*
story	*account*	*narrative*	*tale*
strange	*odd*	*peculiar*	*weird*
take	*hold*	*possess*	*grasp*
tell	*reveal*	*show*	*state*
think	*consider*	*ponder*	*reflect*
trouble	*distress*	*torture*	*wretchedness*
true	*correct*	*right*	*exact*
ugly	*dreadful*	*hideous*	*monstrous*

VERBS

*There are two types of **action verbs** – **physical verbs** and **mental verbs**. **Physical verbs** usually describe an action someone or something does physically.*

Examples of physical verbs:

act	answer	break	build
buy	cough	create	cry
dance	describe	draw	drink
eat	enter	invent	jump
laugh	listen	paint	play
read	run	scream	shout
sing	skip	sleep	sneeze
teach	touch	turn	walk
win	write	whistle	yawn

Verbs describing mental actions do exactly that – describe things which don't happen to you physically, only things take place in your mind instead...

Examples of mental verbs

decide	dislike	doubt	feel
forget	hate	hope	know
learn	like	look	love
mind	notice	own	realise
recognise	remember	suspect	surprise
please	promise	think	understand

There are hundreds and hundreds of ***powerful action verbs*** which you can use in your writing to help it to take off and fly. However, to make it easier for you to choose the right one, I have compiled the following lists for you, trying to group them together so that it makes the process of picking the prefect ***powerful action verb*** that much easier for you...

Examples of verbs you can use to show feelings or emotions: accept ache admire affect agonise alarm alienate amaze amuse, annoy appall betray bless bore brave calm challenge cheer comfort concern confide consider crush cry dare deject delight deprive desire despair determine detest devote diminish disappoint discourage disgust disillusion disinterest dislike dismay dissatisfy distress distrust dominate doubt dread embarrass encourage engross enjoy enrage enthuse excite fascinate fear force frighten frown frustrate fume grieve grin hate hesitate hope humiliate incense inflame infuriate injure inspire insult intend interest irritate laugh liberate like loathe lose love menace motivate mourn need offend overjoy pain panic paralyse perplex please prefer provoke quiet reassure rebel reinforce reject relax rely resent reserve respect satisfy scare secure sigh smile smirk sulk surprise suspect sympathise terrify thank threaten thrill torment torture touch tremble understand upset victimise want warm weep wince wish worry

Examples of verbs you can use to show movement: advance aim amble angle back-away bolt bounce bound canter careen career carry charge crawl creep dance dart dash dawdle dive emerge escape flee flop flounce fly gallop glide go hasten head hike hit hop journey hurry hurtle jaunt jog journey jump labour leap limp lunge march meander mooch mosey move nip pace plod potter pound prance proceed progress prowl pull push race ramble return roam roll run rush saunter scamper scarper scoot scud scuff scurry scuttle shake shuffle slide slink slip slither sneak speed spin sprint stagger stalk step streak stride stroll strut stumble swagger sweep tap throw tiptoe traipse trample travel tread trip troop trot trudge trundle tumble turn undulate waddle walk wander wave wend whizz wind wobble zoom

Examples of verbs you can use for changing objects or things: bend break burn close coil control crush dissolve fold melt mend mould open repair scorch smash snap stretch tear twist wrinkle

Examples of verbs you can use to show thoughts: believe comprehend consider daydream decide dream envisage evaluate expect feel forget gauge guess idea imagine know lament meditate notice ponder realise recall reflect remember sense speculate suppose think understand visualise wonder

Examples of verbs you can use for the senses: caress detect eat feel foretaste glimpse grasp hear heed inhale know lick listen look notice observe perceive smell sniff stare taste touch watch

Examples of verbs you can use to show ways of speaking: address admit advise agree analyse appeal argue ask assure babble bark bawl beg bellow bemoan blabber bleat blubber bluff blurt bluster boast brag breathe cackle call chant chatter cheer chortle chuckle clarify coax comment complain concede confess confide confirm consent convey correct cough crow cry decide declare demand describe disagree drawl drone entreat exclaim expand explain express falter forward fuss giggle goad groan growl grumble grunt hint hiss holler hoot howl hum illustrate inform insist interrupt jabber judge laud laugh lecture lie mention mislead moan mouth mumble murmur mutter nag narrate observe offer order outline pant parrot persuade pester plead prattle preach query question quote ramble rant rebuff recall recommend recount refuse rejoin repeat reply report respond retort reveal roar sass say scold scream screech shout shriek sigh sing slur snap snarl snicker sniff snigger snivel sob speak spit spout sputter squawk squeak squeal stammer state stutter submit suggest summarise summon tattle taunt tease tell urge vocalise voice wail warble weep whimper whine whisper whistle wonder yammer yap yawn yell yelp

VERB ALTERNATIVES

*Want to vary your **verb** vocabulary but not sure which other **verb** to swap it for? Never fear – here's another quick guide to help you switch your **verbs** around. However, remember to use a **thesaurus** to check it's the correct word to choose and substitute the original **verb** with.*
(SEE ALSO SYNONYMS and VERBS)

AGREE – *accept acknowledge consent obey nod*

APPEAR – *arise arrive bloom develop emerge flash manifest materialise show spawn surface*

ASK - *cross-examine demand grill inquire interrogate plead pose query question quiz request*

ATTACK – *ambush assault barrage batter battle beat bombard charge clobber combat overwhelm raid rush storm strike*

ATTEMPT – *chance embark gamble seek strive tackle try undertake venture*

BREAK – *break burst bust carve chop cleave crack cut damage divide explode fracture fragment hack halve rupture sever shatter slit smash snap splinter split tear*

BRING – *carry convey fetch gather guide import lug pick up retrieve return*

BUILD – *construct create erect form fortify layer raise reinforce shape stack*

BUMP – *clatter jar jolt jostle knock nudge slam strike tap thump whack*

CALL – *bawl bellow cry exclaim hail holler proclaim request roar scream shout signal summon yell*

CHANGE – *adapt adjust alter blur distort evolve fluctuate modify mutate reform shift switch transform twist vary warp*

CHASE – *follow hound hunt pursue shadow stalk track trail*

CHOOSE – *determine draw opt for pick pluck prefer select vote*

CLIMB – *ascend heave mount rise scale scramble shimmy*

CLOSE – *batten down cage fasten fold lock down plug seal secure sheathe shut shutter slam*

COLLECT – *accrue amass compile garner gather group harvest* *hoard reap save scrape stockpile store*

COME – *advance appear approach arrive attend converge enter meet*

CROSS – *bridge ford glide pass traverse*

CRY – *bawl bray call cheer holler howl mewl roar scream screech shout shriek squeal trill wail whimper whoop yell yelp*

CUT – *axe carve chip chop cleave crop dissect divide hack hew nick pierce prune saw score sever shave shear slash slice snip split tear trim*

DIG – *burrow core delve dredge drill excavate exhume gouge hollow mine tunnel unearth*

ENTER – *access barge-in board burst intrude invade penetrate pierce trespass wander*

FALL – *buckle collapse crash crumple dive drop pitch plummet plunge sink slant slip slump spill stumble topple tumble trip*

FIGHT – *assault attack battle brawl clash duel feud grapple quarrel scrap scuffle skirmish spar struggle tussle war wrestle*

FIND – *acquire catch detect discover locate notice obtain reveal solve uncover unearth*

FIT – *apply arrange blend cram force implant jam lock mould nest pack place pound press stuff wedge*

FIX –*correct cure improve maintain mend patch rebuild refit renovate repair restore tinker*

GET – *accomplish acquire attain catch earn extract fetch gain gather inherit obtain reap receive secure take win*

GIVE – *award bequeath bestow confer deliver distribute donate gift grant hand offer pass present sacrifice toss*

GRAB – *apprehend arrest catch claim clutch grapple grip hook net nick pluck seize snag snatch steal take trap wrench*

HELP – *advise aid assist befriend boost comfort encourage guide heal intercede nurture relieve save serve support*

HIDE – *blanket bury camouflage cloak clothe cloud conceal cover curtain disguise enclose envelop film hide mask obscure protect screen seal shade shelter shield shroud smother smuggle stash stow veil wrap*

HIT – *bash beat bump clap clobber deck knock poke pound punch slam slap slash smack strike swat swing wallop whack*
HOLD –*carry clasp clench clutch cradle grasp grip handle shelter shoulder squeeze support*
HURRY – *advance bolt bustle cruise dash glide hasten hustle quicken rush scamper scurry scuttle slide speed sweep zip*
JOIN – *add attach blend bridge cement combine couple fasten fuse glue graft hinge knit link marry merge pair pin splice staple stitch tether unite weave weld*
JUMP – *bounce bound hop hurdle leap leapfrog lurch pounce skip spring surge vault*
KNOW – *detect feel identify perceive realise sense understand*
LEAVE – *abandon avoid away bail bolt clear depart disappear ditch elude escape evacuate evade exit flee forsake quit retire run scramble sidestep sneak split vacate withdraw*
LIFT – *boost elevate heave heft hike hoist raise rise winch*
LISTEN –*eavesdrop hear heed mind monitor overhear*
LOOK – *attend behold browse contemplate detect examine follow gawk glance glimpse inspect leer monitor note notice observe peek peep regard scan scope scrutinise see seek spy squint stare survey view watch witness*
MAKE – *assemble combine create design fashion forge form invent mould produce sculpt shape*
MOVE – *budge displace fiddle jar jiggle manouevre nudge position relocate shift slide tap work*
NEED – *ache claim covet crave demand desire dream hunger pine require thirst want wish yearn*
OPEN – *bare expand expose free peel release reveal spread unbolt uncork uncover undo unfasten unfold unfurl unhinge unlock unzip widen*
PLAY – *act cavort clown dabble dally entertain flirt frisk frolic joke rejoice romp tease toy*
PICK – *bag clasp collect cull gather grasp harvest hook pluck select*
PULL – *draw drag haul lug tow transport trawl tug yank*

PUSH – *bulldoze crowd crush drive elbow encourage force jostle knock muscle nudge poke press prod propel shove squish thrust*
PUT– *deposit drop lay lodge nest place plant position rest seat settle spread*
REMEMBER – *daydream flashback recall recognise recollect reminisce revive*
RIDE – *coast cruise gallop glide jockey mount speed surf*
RUN – *amble barrel canter dart dash flee fly gallop hustle jet jog pelt race rush scamper scoot scurry scuttle speed sprint stampede trot*
SAY – *address articulate banter chant chat converse curse dictate discuss drone murmur rant rave snarl speak stammer stutter swear whisper yell **(SEE ALSO SAID ALTERNATIVES)***
SEARCH – *browse delve dig examine explore ferret forage hunt investigate probe pursue quest ransack rummage scout seek sift*
SEND – *broadcast cast channel publish radiate relay route ship transfer transmit volley*
SHAKE – *convulse flutter jerk jolt judder lurch quake quaver quiver rattle ripple shiver shudder slosh spasm squirm thrash throb tremble tremor twinge twitch vibrate*
SIT – *crouch flop huddle laze lounge park perch recline relax rest roost settle slouch sprawl squat straddle*
START – *activate begin birth dawn embark enter erupt initiate jump launch plunge sally set out spring*
STOP –*cease conclude discontinue end finish freeze halt hitch hold pause quit refrain rein retire stall suspend terminate*
THINK - *consider debate doubt dwell ponder puzzle question speculate study wonder*
THROW - *catapult chuck discharge fire fling flip heave hurl launch lob pelt propel sling thrust toss volley*
TRAP – *bind cage capture catch chain clutch corner handcuff hold imprison pin pinch restrain shackle snare snatch surround*
TURN – *bend circle crank curl fork lean loop pivot revolve rotate spin sway swerve swing swirl switch swivel tilt twist twirl*
USE – *adopt manipulate operate practice utilise wield work*

VISIT – *attend court frequent haunt tour*
WAIT – *adhere bide dally delay dwell hesitate hold hover idle linger loiter pause remain settle stand stay tarry*
WALK – *amble clomp clump creep glide limp lumber lurch march pace pad parade plod prowl roam saunter scamper shuffle slink slog sneak stamp stride stroll strut swagger tiptoe toddle totter trample trudge waddle*
WASH – *bathe cleanse clean lather launder rinse scour scrub shampoo shower sluice soak soap swab*
WHISPER – *confide-in mouth mumble murmur mutter wheeze*

JONAS LANE'S HELPFUL HINTS ON SPELLINGS

"The English language is full of words that are just waiting to be misspelled, and the world is full of sticklers, ready to pounce."
— *Mary Norris*

"'I' before 'E' except after 'C', and when sounded like 'ay' as in neighbor and weigh, and on weekends and holidays, and all throughout May, and you'll always be wrong no matter what you say!"
— *Brian Regan*

SPELLINGS AND SPELLING RULES YOU ARE SUPPOSED TO KNOW BY THE END OF KEY STAGE 2

*Lots of the spellings and spelling rules you will have been taught or need to know by the time you go to secondary school we've already touched upon earlier in this book in the sections **ADVERBS**, **HOMOPHONES**, **HYPHENS**, **MNEMONICS**, **PREFIXES** and **SUFFIXES**. The following pages provide you with lists and examples of all the others you should either know or be able to find in a really magical spell book called a **dictionary** (sorry, Poppy Copperthwaite!)*

Examples of words beginning with the prefixes *dis-*, *mis-*, *in-*, *il-*, *im-*, *ir-*, *re-*, *sub-*, *inter-*, *super-*, *anti-*, *auto-*: dismay misinform, in appropriate illegal impossible irregular recall submarine international superstar antifreeze autobiography

(SEE ALSO PREFIXES)

Examples of words ending with the suffix *-acy* or*-cy* meaning *state* or *quality*: democracy fluency literacy numeracy privacy

Examples of words ending with the suffix *-ance* or *ence* meaning *state* or *quality of*: coincidence dominance maintenance prominence

Examples of words ending with the suffix *-ate* meaning *become*: complicate dedicate demonstrate eradicate hesitate moderate

Examples of words ending with the suffix *-ation* meaning *act or process*: alliteration compilation dedication desperation duration information inspiration moderation resignation starvation

Examples of words ending with the suffix *-er*, *-or* or *-eer* meaning *one who is/does, that which is/does*: butcher clippers doctor engineer hoover mentor pioneer survivor teacher toaster

Examples of words ending with the suffix *-ed* meaning *in the past (past-tense verbs)*: *hunted jumped played skipped turned*

Examples of words ending with the suffix *-en* meaning *to become* or *to make*: *fasten golden heighten straighten tighten wooden*

Examples of words ending with the suffix *-er* meaning *more* or *less*: *faster fitter greater harder louder older slower taller younger*

Examples of words ending with the suffix *-est* also meaning *more* or *less*: *greatest hardest hottest loudest oldest poorest saddest*

Examples of words ending with the suffix *-ful* meaning *full of*: *cheerful colourful delightful forgetful hateful helpful painful peaceful playful restful spiteful stressful truthful useful wishful*

Examples of words ending with the suffix *-graph* meaning *to write/be written*: *autograph autobiography biography photograph telegraph*

Examples of words ending with the suffix *-ian* or *-cian* meaning *one who is/does*: *electrician librarian magician physician technician*

Examples of words ending with the suffix *-ied* meaning *in the past (past-tense verbs)*: *copied defied denied supplied replied*

Examples of words ending with the suffix *-ier* meaning *more* or *less*: *angrier grumpier happier moodier sunnier wealthier*

Examples of words ending with the suffix *-ier* meaning *one who is* or *one that/which does*: *barrier brazier carrier copier cashier*

Examples of words ending with the suffix *-ify* or *-fy* meaning *to make* or *to become*: clarify classify defy magnify rectify simplify terrify

Examples of words ending with the suffix *-ing* meaning *in the present* or *action/process*: catching eating helping hiking hopping jumping laughing painting running sailing shopping shouting skating swimming throwing walking

Examples of words ending with the suffix *-ion, -sion, -ssion* or *-tion meaning state/condition/action/process* or *result of*: action conclusion concussion description erosion explanation invitation possession relation revolution starvation transition vision
(*SEE ALSO -ation, -ian and -cian*)

Examples of words ending with the suffix *-ist* meaning *one who makes* or *does*: artist chemist dentist motorist scientist

Examples of words ending with the suffix *-ise* meaning *to cause* or *to become:* alphabetise apologise capitalise categorise chastise, criticise energise hypnotise magnetise modernise summarise

Examples of words ending with the suffix *-ity* or *-ty* meaning *state, quality* or *condition of*: ability activity beauty certainty curiosity generosity hostility locality possibility quality

Examples of words ending with the suffix *-ive* meaning *having the nature of*: conclusive creative effective executive festive instructive inventive negative positive responsive

Examples of words ending with the suffix *-less* meaning *without*: careless endless fearless harmless homeless lifeless powerless selfless tasteless thoughtless worthless

Examples of words ending with the suffix *-ly* meaning *characteristic of* or *in what manner*: bravely carefully cowardly easily firstly happily hourly loudly majestically nicely nonchalantly quickly rarely rudely softly sweetly wisely
(SEE ALSO ADVERBS ENDING -LY)

Examples of words ending with the suffix *-ment* meaning *action, condition, result* or *process of*: amazement argument basement development disappointment embarrassment encouragement engagement enjoyment entertainment excitement punishment replacement retirement

Examples of words ending with the suffix *-ness* meaning *state* or *condition of*: awareness awkwardness boldness calmness carelessness cleanliness, darkness eagerness emptiness fairness fitness goodness happiness helpfulness illness likeness quietness sadness shyness tightness

Examples of words ending with the suffix *-ology* meaning *the study* or *science of*: archaeology biology ecology geology mythology technology terminology theology

Examples of words ending with the suffix *-ous or -ious* meaning *having the qualities of* or *full of*: adventurous anonymous courageous curious, dangerous disastrous enormous fabulous furious humorous jealous mischievous momentous mountainous nervous poisonous ridiculous thunderous victorious

Examples of words ending with the suffix with the suffix *-port* meaning *to carry*: deport export import report transport

Examples of words ending with the suffixes *-s, -es, or ies* meaning *more than one*: babies boxes cars copies diaries fairies foxes hotels houses planets ponies prefixes suffixes toys wishes

Examples of words ending with the suffix -y meaning *characterised by* or *somewhat like*: *chilly cloudy crazy curly dusty faulty fiery foggy funny glossy heavenly noisy nosey oily risky shiny*

Examples of words spelt with the letters *ph* which make the *f sound* when spoken: *alphabet atmosphere biography dolphin elephant phantom phase phone photograph phase phrase physical sophisticated telephone*

Examples of words with the *letter y* in the middle that sound like the *letter i* when spoken: *calypso crypt crystal hymn lyric mystery myth oxygen rhythm symbol symptom system typical*

Examples of words containing the *letters ou* which sound like the *letter u* when spoken: *country couple courage cousin double encourage enough rough touch tough trouble young*

Examples of words ending with *-sure* and *-ture*: *adventure architecture assure composure creature culture fracture furniture gesture lecture leisure measure misadventure mixture moisture nature picture pleasure pressure puncture sculpture temperature treasure unsure*

WARNING!

As always, there is an exception to this rule... Some words sound like they should end *–ture*, but check to see if the **root word** ends with either the letters **ch** or **tch** first as the **suffix -er** is then added instead...

Examples of words which would then be spelt this way: *ar**ch**er tea**ch**er prea**ch**er ca**tch**er tha**tch**er ri**ch**er stre**tch**er.*

Examples of words ending with *-tion* *-sion* *-ssion* or *-cian* which make the word end with a *shun* sound when spoken: *action admission affection attention collection collision conclusion confession confusion education electrician fiction information*

141

musician observation obsession optician passion percussion population possession profession proportion punctuation revolution subtraction tension

(SEE ALSO SUFFIXES)

Examples of words ending with the letters *al, el* **or** *le: aisle approval, bicycle capital channel gradual kettle legal magical medical parallel parcel tunnel uncle*

Examples of words spelt with the *letters ch* **but which sound like the** *letter k* **or** *letters sh* **when spoken:** *ache achilles alchemist anchor arachnid archaeology archangel architect architectural backache bellyache chameleon chaos chaotic chaotically character charismatic chasm chemical chemistry choir cholera chorus chronological echo headache heartache leprechaun mechanical monarch orchestra orchid psycho scheme school stomach technical technology uncharacteristic*

Examples of words spelt with the *letters sc* **but sound like the letter** *s* **when spoken:** *abscess adolescent ascend descend disciple fascinate fascination isosceles miscellaneous muscle obscene scene scent science scissors*

Examples of words ending with *-gue* **and** *–que: antique catalogue cheque dialogue frequent guess, guest infrequent league lounge question queue tongue unique vague*

Examples of words which are *homophones (sounding the same but spelt differently)***:** *bare bear blew blue by bye knew new their there they're threw through to too two wander wonder ware wear where weather whether witch which whose who's*

(SEE ALSO HOMOPHONES SECTION).

Examples of words ending with *-cious* **and** *-tious: ambitious atrocious cautious conscious delicious ferocious fictitious* *gracious infectious luscious malicious precious scrumptious spacious superstitious suspicious unconscious vicious*

Examples of words ending with *-cial* **and** *-tial*: *artificial confidential crucial essential facial financial initial partial potential racial social special substantial torrential*

Examples of words ending with *-ent* **and** *-ant*: *accident ancient apparent argument arrogant brilliant comment different elegant elephant extravagant giant inhabitant instrument obedient present relevant rodent silent talent*

Examples words ending with *-ance, -ancy, -ence* **or** *ency*: *confidence currency decency difference hindrance intelligence performance reference resistance tendency vacancy*

Examples of words ending with *-able, -ably, -ible* **or** *-ibly*: *adorable arguably comfortably considerably dependable edible horribly identifiable impossibly incredibly miserably noticeably possible predictable predictably probable reliable responsibly reversible sensible suitably terrible unacceptable unbelievably uncomfortable understandably vegetable visible*

Examples of words containing *-ough* **which sound like the have the** *ow*, *uff* **or** *or* **sounds when spoken**: *around borough bough bought brought enough fought ground plough pound round sound tough*

Examples of words using *hyphens*: *call-up check-in clean-cut co-operate co-ordinate, double-cross high-tech know-it-all left-handed quick-witted round-trip single-minded strong-arm x-ray*
(SEE ALSO HYPHENS SECTION)

Examples of words with the *sh* **sound in them which are spelt differently**: *brochures chef crashed issue machine moustache* *parachutes pressure session sugar tissue*

Examples of words spelt with the *ay* sound which are also spelt differently: *afraid bake break change claims complain great migrate obey raining reindeer sleigh snail survey train weigh*

Examples of words ending with -en or -on: *baton broaden button canyon children citizen garden golden horizon molten opinion prison rotten skeleton soften spoken stallion stolen weapon wooden woollen*

(SEE ALSO SUFFIXES)

Examples of words with *silent letters* in them: *campaign chemist crescent crumbs debt doubt exhaust fascinating gnarled gnaw gnomes handsome island knife knight knot know knuckle limb rhinoceros rhubarb rhyme salmon science scissors subtle sword thistle tomb whale where wrench wrestle wrinkles wrong*

Examples of words spelt with *ei* and *ie*: *achievement ancient ceiling deceive field friends glacier neighbour perceive receipt receive seize society weight*

WARNING
The *i* before *e* spelling rule....
If, like me, you've been taught the ***i before e except after c*** rhyme to help remember these types of spellings so that you don't get the two letters the wrong way around, you'll be surprised to know that it's not actually the entire saying...

*"i before **e**,
except after **c** or when sounded as **a**,
as in n**ei**ghbour and w**ei**gh.
And w**ei**rd is just w**ei**rd!*

As you can see from above, the ***i before e except after c*** rule isn't always true. It's useful in helping us to remember some

144

spellings, but there are exceptions to this rule....

- **When sounded as *ay* as in the words like *neighbour* and *weigh***

When a word has the ***ay sound*** in them, the letter *e* comes before the *i*.

Examples
eight neighbour weigh veil veins

- **When sounded as *eye* as in *Einstein***

When a word has an ***eye sound*** in them, the **letter e** comes before the ***letter i*** again.

Examples
Liechtenstein eiderdown Frankenstein Oppenheimer stein glass

- **Words that are often mistaken as exceptions but which are actually spelt correctly.**

There are quite a few other words which do not follow the *i before except after c... rule* but which are spelt correctly. Unfortunately, there isn't an easy way to remember these words so keep checking this book if you're uncertain!

Examples
either foreign forfeit height leisure neither seize weight weird

- **Words which contain -*cien***

Words containing the letters -*cien* also do not follow the *i before except after c... rule* either but are spelt correctly.

Examples
ancient conscience efficient science sufficient

SPELLINGS – THE FIRST 300 HIGH FREQUENCY WORDS YOU NEED TO KNOW HOW TO SPELL

According to the Department for Education, these are the first 300 high frequency words you will have used when speaking or writing at school which you should know how to easily spell.
See how many of these are you able to confidently spell correctly without checking...

A - a about across after again air all along am an and animals another any are around as asked at away

B- baby back bad be bear because bed been before began best better big birds boat book box boy but by

C - called came can can't car cat children clothes cold come coming could couldn't cried

D - dad dark day did didn't different do dog don't door down dragon duck

E - each eat eggs end even ever every everyone eyes

F - fast feet fell find first fish floppy fly food for found fox friends from fun

G - garden gave get giant girl go going gone good got gran grandad great green grow

H - had hard has hat have he he's head help her here him his home horse hot house how

I - I I'll I'm I've if in inside into is it it's its

J - jumped just

K - keep key king know

L - last laughed let let's like liked little live lived long look looked looking looks lots

M - made magic make man many may me miss more morning most mother mouse Mr Mrs much mum must my

N - narrator need never new next night no not now

O - of off oh old on once one only or other our out over

P - park people place plants play please pulled put

Q - queen

R - rabbit ran really red right river room round run

S - said sat saw say school sea see she shouted sleep small snow so some something soon still stop stopped suddenly sun

T - take tea tell than that that's the their them then there there's these they thing things think this thought three through time to told too took top town tree trees two

U - under up us use very

W - want wanted was water way we we're well went were what when where which white who why will wind window wish with work would

Y - yes you your

SPELLINGS – THE WORDS YOU NEED TO KNOW HOW TO SPELL BY THE END OF KEY STAGE 2

*Finally, here are the spellings the Department for Educations say you should know how to also spell by the end of Year 4 (in ITALICS) and by the end of Year 6 in **BOLD**).*

A *– accident accidentally actual actually address although answer appear arrive* **accommodate accompany according achieve aggressive amateur ancient apparent appreciate attached available average awkward**

B *- believe bicycle breath breathe build busy/business* **bargain bruise**

C *- calendar caught centre century certain circle complete consider continue* **category cemetery committee communicate community competition conscience conscious controversy convenience correspond criticise curiosity**

D *- decide describe different difficult disappear* **definite desperate determined develop dictionary disastrous**

E *- early earth eight/eighth enough exercise experience experiment extreme* **embarrass environment equip equipped equipment) especially exaggerate excellent existence explanation**

F - famous favourite February forward forwards fruit **familiar foreign forty frequently**

G - grammar group guard guide **government guarantee**

H - heard heart height history **harass hindrance**

I - imagine increase important interest island **identity immediate immediately individual interfere interrupt**

K - knowledge

L - learn length library **language leisure lightning**

M - material medicine mention minute **marvellous mischievous muscle**

N - natural naughty notice **necessary neighbour nuisance**

O – occasion occasionally often opposite ordinary **occupy occur opportunity**

P - particular peculiar perhaps popular position possess possession possible potatoes pressure probably promise purpose **parliament persuade physical prejudice privilege profession programme pronunciation**

Q - quarter question **queue**

R - recent regular reign remember **recognise recommend relevant restaurant rhyme rhythm**

S - sentence separate special straight strange strength suppose surprise **sacrifice secretary shoulder signature sincere sincerely soldier stomach sufficient suggest symbol system**

T – therefore though thought through **temperature thorough twelfth**

V, X & Y - various **variety vegetable vehicle** *weight woman women* **yacht**

JONAS LANE SAYS "*CHECK IT OUT NOW!*" WITH THESE HELPFUL CHECKLISTS FOR YOUNG WRITERS...

"Writing is a skill, not a talent and this difference is important because a skill can be improved by practice."
— *Robert Stacy McCain*

"Learn the rules like a pro so that you can break them like an artist..."
— *Pablo Picasso*

A CHECKLIST WHEN WRITING FOR THE PURPOSE OF ENTERTAINING OTHERS

*Rather than have checklist after checklist for every piece of writing you do, I prefer to use these four main ones with my students or young writers, inspired by Michael Tidd and based upon the **purposes** writers use for writing - to **create a literary work**, to **express themselves**, to **inform** or to **persuade** their readers...*
First, writing to entertain the reader...

These types of texts include... Narratives including Story extracts, Stories (including recounts and re-tellings) Character/setting descriptions, Poetry, Playscripts, Written pieces in character or role play including Diaries, Blogs, Journals, Monologues etc.

Text Features
First, check to see if your writing needs and has the following text features for what you've been writing.

Narratives/stories etc.
*Is your narrative/story time sequenced and organised in clearly defined **paragraphs** showing changes of **place**, **time**, **speaker** or **perspective**?*
Does your narrative/story have:
- *an **introduction** which grabs or hooks the interest of the reader?*
- *a **build-up** with a problem or issue?*
- *a **dilemma** shown by words like 'perhaps' or 'maybe'?*
- *an exciting part or a **problem**?*
- *a **resolution** where the problem is solved?*
- *suspense or tension which builds towards a dramatic action sequence or climax?*
- *a clear **ending** which either links back to the introduction or ends with a cliffhanger/surprise for the reader?*

Does your story describe objects, items or traditions which are appropriate for other cultures, countries, time periods or fantasy worlds?

Is your narrative set in an imaginary place, time or world and have make-believe or mythical characters and/or creatures?

Poetry

*Does it have a **title**?*

*Does your poem have an appropriate **pattern** or **rhythm**?*

Has it a clear and consistent rhyme scheme? e.g. lines 2 and 4 rhyme, rhyming couplets etc.

*Have you written your poem using **stanzas**, **verses** or **lines**?*

Playscripts

*Does it have a **title**?*

Have you listed the characters at the beginning?

*Are the characters' names written on the left and have a **colon** after each?*

Have you introduced and described your opening scene? (where/when etc.)

Have you started a new line for every new speaker?

*Are your stage directions written in **brackets ( )** and in the **present tense**?*

*Have you given **stage directions** as to how the actors must speak or move?*

Every time the setting changes (place or time) have you started a new scene?

*Have you used **ellipsis** (...) to show when a character is thinking or stuttering?*

*Have used **CAPITALS** or **italics** to emphasise words or stage directions?*

*Does your play script have **acts**? (Act 1 beginning, Act 2 middle, Act 3 End etc.)*

*Have you remembered not to use **speech marks/inverted commas**?*

Next, check your grammar and the sentences you've written...

Does your writing have or need a *title*?

Have you included *fronted adverbials* showing *how/where/when* etc.?

Have you used a range of different *sentence starters* throughout? e.g. *fronted adverbials, prepositional phrases, -ing and -ed clauses, similes etc.*

Have you used *specific nouns* and ambitious *adjectives* to create imagery and atmosphere?

Are there any *noun/expanded noun phrases* included to add both detail and description?

Have you used *prepositional phrases* to show *time, manner, frequency* or *place* to help explain the action and improve your descriptions?

Have you used *specific verbs* which help to further enhance meaning?

Did you vary the position of *adverbials* within sentences for effect? e.g. *as a sentence starter/at the end of a sentence*?

Have you used both *relative* and *subordinate clauses* in different positions to add extra detail or context?

Have you used *adjectives* and *adjectival phrases* to help create atmosphere and to build tension?

Is there *ambitious language* included to describe characters and settings? e.g. well-chosen *adjectives, adverbs, powerful verbs etc.*

Have you used a range of *figurative language* to improve descriptions of characters and settings? e.g. *alliteration, metaphors, similes, personification, onomatopoeia, repetition etc.*

Have you used your five senses to describe what the characters *see, hear, smell, touch or feel*?

Are there a range of *coordinating conjunctions* which link two main ideas or *paragraphs* together?

Have you used a mixture of *nouns* and *pronouns* for *clarity* and *cohesion*?

Is there a range of *emotive language* used to show how your characters are feeling?

Have you included *direct* or *reported speech* to help move the narrative forward with well-chosen *speech verbs* and *adverbs* used to help improve meaning?

Have you used the *Rule of three/Power of three* in your sentences to help describe *action, characters* and/or *settings*?

Have you used different sentence structures – *simple, compound and complex*?

Did you also vary the length of your sentences for extra effect? e.g. *short for impact, longer for setting/describing the scene etc.?*

Have you used *exclamation sentences* where appropriate?

Have you included *rhetorical questions* to engage the reader and show a character/narrator's thoughts?

Did you use *show not tell* techniques to describe characters and *infer* how they are feeling/speaking?

Is it written in the correct *tense* throughout or have you used a range of *tenses* to indicate changes in *timing, sequence* etc.?

Have you stayed in the same narrative voice throughout? e.g. *1st 2nd or 3rd person*

Have you *read aloud* your sentences to check that they make complete sense to the reader?

Is your finished piece of writing *cohesive*? Does it *flow*?

Now check for all the punctuation you could have used...

Are *capital letters* used at the *start of* - and *full stops* used at the *end of* - *each sentence*?

Have you used *capital letters* for *proper nouns/the pronoun I?*

Are there *commas* after *fronted adverbials*, for *parenthesis*, for lists and/or for *subordinate clauses*?

Have you also used *commas* - along with *brackets* or *dashes* - for emphasis, *parenthesis* or incidentals?

Have you used *apostrophes* for contraction?

Have you also used *apostrophes* to show possession, including for *plural nouns*?

Have you used *exclamation marks*, especially when relating to speech?

Have you also used *question marks* in speech and for *rhetorical questions*?

Have *speech marks* been used correctly and are accurately punctuated before and within the *inverted commas*?

Have you attempted to use other higher-level *punctuation* for effect? e.g. *ellipsis, hyphens* etc.

Have you used *semi-colons* to either join related *clauses* or when needed and appropriate?

Have you used *colons* correctly? e.g. to add further detail in a new *clause*

Time to check your handwriting carefully...

Is your *handwriting joined* and *legible?*

Have you checked to make sure that you have not joined any of your *capital letters* to the rest of your writing?

Are all of your letters the *correct shape* and *size*?

Have you written your *ascenders* and *descenders* correctly?

Finally, make sure you check all of your spellings...

Have you checked you have spelt all common *homophones* correctly?

Are all the *high frequency words* you have learned or used from the *Year 3 & 4* and/or *Year 5 & 6 lists* spelt correctly?

Have you checked to make sure you have remembered your spelling rules when changing a word to a *plural,* or adding a *suffix* etc.?

Have you used a *dictionary* to check the spelling of any *ambitious, technical, historical, scientific* or *challenging vocabulary included?*

Have you used a *thesaurus* to check the meaning of a word before substituting it?

A CHECKLIST WHEN WRITING FOR THE PURPOSE OF INFORMING OTHERS

These types of tests include... Autobiography/Biographies, Explanations, Journals, Diaries, Blogs, Event Write-ups, Reports, Recounts, Letters, Instructions

Text Features:
First, check to see if your writing needs and has the following text features for what you've been writing.

General features required of information texts:
Does it have an **introduction** that hooks the reader? e.g. *factual statement/opening question etc.*

Is there a **middle section** with **paragraphs** which use your topic sentences or *subheadings* (if required)?

Have you summed up your piece with an **ending/summary/conclusion** etc. followed by a **personal comment/warning/question** etc.)

Instructions:
Does the text tell you what to do – **one step at a time** - and what **equipment and/or ingredients** you need?

Is it written in **simple, easy to understand** language?

Have you used **numbers?** (1, 2, 3, 4 etc.)

Does it have **labelled diagrams?**

Have you used any other different techniques to **highlight** key words? *(bold, underlined, etc.)*

Is your text built around a **key image/includes images?**

Autobiography/Biography:
Is it clear **who** the writing is about?

Does the text give you **factual information** about the person and **events** in their life?

Is it in **chronological order** with **dates** to show when the *events* took place?

Letter:
Does your letter use a *friendly* writing style (*informal letter*) or a *formal* writing style? (*formal letter*)
Have you written the *date* and the sender's *address*?
Have you written an appropriate *salutation* or *greeting*? (Dear/To etc.)
Does your letter address the *recipient* directly?
Have you written your ending based on the letter's level of *formality*? (*Your Sincerely/Yours Truly/Yours faithfully/Best wishes/Lots of love...etc.*)
Have you used a *complimentary close*?
Have you finished your letter with the sender's *name* or *signature*?

Diary:
Are there *dates* at the start of each entry?
Have you *addressed* the diary directly as though confiding in/speaking to it?

Non-chronological reports:
Have you used *factual language* and included extra detail to support the main points?
Have you included a *glossary* to explain any *historical, technical, topical* or *scientific detail*?

Newspaper Reports:
Have you included a *headline*?
Have you included other newspaper features? e.g. *byline, photos/pictures captions, quotes, age, addresses* etc.
Have you used the **5 Ws**? (*Who* is it about? *What* happened? *Why* did this happen? *Where* did it happen? *When* did it happen?)

Blog:
Does your blog tell the story of an *episode* in the writer's life? Does it include *events, personal feelings, reactions* and *opinions* which are important to the writer?

Next, check your grammar and the sentences you've written...
Is the *title* included and does it tell you what is to be achieved, who it's about, the whole subject of your report etc.?

Have you used a range of *fronted adverbials* to start your sentences with?

Have you used *expanded noun phrases* which inform the reader?

Are there *topic sentences* used to open *paragraphs*?

Have you used *coordinating conjunctions* to link two main *thoughts* or *ideas*?

Have you used *subordinating conjunctions* to join *clauses*, including being used as *openers*?

Have you also used *subordinating conjunctions* in different positions in your *sentences*?

Have you used *factual language* where needed?

Have you used *adverbials* and *prepositions* to *add detail, open sentences* and for extra *cohesion* across your sentences?

Are there a range of different *synonyms* and *pronouns* used to help avoid accidental *repetition*?

Have you used *generalisers* like *most...some...many* etc. for additional information?

Used *relative clauses* to add further detail to your writing?

Have you varied the length of your *sentences* to suit the *purpose* of your writing?

Have you tried to use the *passive voice* when trying to stay *formal* or *detached*?

Is it written in the correct *narrative voice* throughout? e.g. *1st person* (*autobiography*) *3rd person* (*biography*) etc.

Have you used *time conjunctions* where necessary, especially when writing in *chronological order?*

Have you used *organisational devices* to structure your text if appropriate? e.g. **sub-headings, fact boxes, bullet points** etc.

Have you used the correct level of *formality*? e.g written as if talking to someone (***informal tone***), writing a newspaper report (***formal tone***) etc.

Have you used both ***reported*** and ***direct speech*** when required?

Have ***imperative – bossy - verbs*** been used if required?

Have you included a range of ***literary devices*** appropriately in your writing? e.g. ***alliteration, metaphors, similes, etc.***

Are ***powerful verbs*** and ***adverbs*** used effectively?

Does it keep the reader interested using *well-chosen words* and *well-chosen* vocabulary?

Are there any ***exclamation sentences*** or ***rhetorical*** questions?

Did you effectively use ***show not tell*** techniques when required?

Have you ***read aloud*** your sentences to check that they make complete sense to the reader?

Is it written in the correct ***tense*** throughout or have a range of ***tenses*** to indicate changes in *timing, sequence*, etc.?

Is your writing ***cohesive***? Does it *flow*?

Now check for all the punctuation you could have used…

Are ***capital letters*** used at the *start of* - and ***full stops*** used at the *end of* - each *sentence*?

Have you used ***capital letters*** for ***proper nouns/the pronoun I?***

Have you used ***paragraph***s to group related ideas?

Are there ***commas*** after ***fronted adverbials***, for ***parenthesis***, for lists and for ***subordinate clauses***?

Have you also used ***commas*** - along with ***brackets*** or ***dashes*** - for emphasis, parenthesis or incidentals?

Have you also used ***brackets*** or ***dashes*** to help you to explain any *historical, technical, topical or scientific vocabulary*?

Have you used ***apostrophes*** for contraction?

Have you also used ***apostrophes*** to show possession, including for ***plural nouns***?

Have you used ***exclamation marks*** appropriately?

Are there **question marks** in speech and for **rhetorical questions**?
Have *speech marks* been used correctly and are accurately punctuated before and within the ***inverted commas***?
Have you attempted to use other higher-level **punctuation** for effect? e.g. ***ellipsis, hyphens*** etc.
Have you used **semi-colons** to either join related **clauses** or when needed and appropriate?
Have you also used **semi-colons** to punctuate complex lists, including when using **bullet points**?
Have you used **colons** correctly? e.g. to add further detail in a new **clause**, to introduce *lists* or *sections* etc.

Time to check your handwriting carefully...
Is your *handwriting **joined*** and ***legible***?
Have you checked to make sure that you have not joined any of your **capital letters** to the rest of your writing?
Are all of your letters the correct *shape* and *size*?
Have you written your **ascenders** and **descenders** correctly?

Finally, make sure that you check all of your spellings...
Have you checked you have spelt all common **homophones** correctly?
Are all the **high frequency words** you have learned or used from the **Year 3 & 4** and/or **Year 5 & 6 lists** spelt correctly?
Have you checked to make sure you have remembered your spelling rules when changing a word to a **plural**, or adding a **suffix** etc.?
Have you used a **dictionary** to check the spelling of any *ambitious, technical, historical, scientific* or *challenging vocabulary* included?
Have you used a **thesaurus** to check the meaning of a word before substituting it?

A CHECKLIST WHEN WRITING FOR THE PURPOSE OF PERSUADING OTHERS

These types of tests include... Advertisements, Persuasive Letters, Debates, Travel brochures, Speeches, Posters, Flyers, Election Campaigns (*Head Boy/Girl, School Council etc.*)

Text Features:
First, check to see if your writing needs and has the following text features for what you've been writing.

General features required of persuasive texts or speeches:
Is the ***point*** of your writing/speech of point of view clearly *explained* and *introduced*?
Have you included a ***hook*** or a ***promise***?
Does it ***address the listener*** directly?
Does it ***acknowledge the argument/accept other viewpoints*** where required?
Have you used ***flattery*** to get them to accept your *opinion* or *point* of view when required?
Does it make use of the ***2nd person***?
Is there deliberate and planned ***repetition***?
Have you included lots of ***facts, figures*** and ***statistics***?
Does it use tempting descriptions of the ***benefits*** you offer?
Does it use intriguing questions to ***entice*** the reader/listener?
Have you used colour and/or included ***photos, colourful pictures drawings*** or ***diagrams*** (especially for advertising)?
Does your completed written ***persuasive text*** have an attractive or eye-catching design?
Is there any *additional* and/or *useful information*, as well as *symbols*, included?
e.g. *opening times, prices/special offers, maps with symbols, location/contact details etc.*
Have you used different ***font styles/sizes*** when required?

Next, check your grammar and the sentences you've written...

Do you have a *title* or *introduction* as to what your *text* or *speech* is about?

Have you used **commands** or **imperative** and/or **modal verbs** to convey a sense of *urgency*?

Are there **noun phrases/expanded noun phrases** to add extra detail and description?

Have you used **appealing** and/or **ambitious adjectives** for *positive feelings* and *descriptions* as required?

Have you used **relative clauses** to provide extra *temptation* to your intended audience?

Have you used a range of different **adverbials** to convey a sense of certainty?

Are there **short, snappy sentences** used for emphasis and effect?

Have you used the **subjunctive form** – *made suggestions to the reader* - for *formal structure*?

Have you included **exclamation sentences**?

Are there **rhetorical questions** to engage the reader or listener?

Have you used **personal pronouns** effectively when addressing your audience?

Have you used **boastful phrases superlatives, exaggeration** and/or **hyperboles** for greater effect?

Have you included a range of **conjunction**s in your writing?

Is it written in the **correct tense** throughout? e.g. *present tense*.

Have you used the **Rule of three/Power of three** to help you strongly put your message across?

Is there **deliberate repetition** to help *emphasise* what you are writing/saying so that your reader/audience remembers the message?

Have you included a catchy *slogan or catchphrase* where needed, using **alliteration, similes, metaphors** or **rhyme?**

Have you included *fronted adverbials, subordinate clauses* and/or **relative clauses?**

Have you used **ambitious** and **persuasive language** throughout?

Have you **read aloud** your sentences to check that they make

complete sense to the reader?
Is your writing **cohesive**? Does it *flow*?

Now check for all the punctuation you could have used...
Are **capital letters** used at the *start of* - and **full stops** used at the *end of* - each sentence?
Have you used **capital letters** for **proper nouns/the pronoun *I*?**
Have you used **paragraph**s to group related points and/or ideas?
Have you included **headings/subheadings** when required?
Are there **commas** after **fronted adverbials**, for **parenthesis**, for lists and for **subordinate clauses**?
Have you also used **commas** - along with **brackets** or **dashes** - for emphasis, **parenthesis** or incidentals?
Have you also used **brackets** or **dashes** to explain *historical, technical, topical* or *scientific vocabulary*?
Have you used **apostrophes** for contraction?
Have you also used **apostrophes** to show possession, including for **plural nouns**?
Have you used **exclamation marks** appropriately?
Are there also **question marks** in speech and for **rhetorical questions**?
Have *speech marks* been used correctly and are accurately punctuated before and within the **inverted commas**?
Have you attempted to use other higher-level **punctuation** for effect? e.g. **ellipsis, hyphens** etc.
Have you used **semi-colons** to either join related **clauses** or when needed and appropriate?
Have you also used **semi-colons** to punctuate complex lists, including when using **bullet points** and to structure **repetition**?
Have you used **colons** correctly? e.g. to add further detail in a new **clause**, to introduce *lists* or *sections* etc.
Have you also used **colons** and **semi-colons** to list features, attractions or arguments when needed?

Time to check your handwriting carefully...
Is your *handwriting joined* and *legible*?
Have you checked to make sure you have not joined any of your *capital letters* to the rest of your writing?
Are all of your letters the correct *shape* and *size*?
Have you written your ***ascenders*** and ***descenders*** correctly?

Finally, make sure that you check all of your spellings...
Have you checked you have spelt all common ***homophones*** correctly?
Are all the ***high frequency words*** you have learned or used from the *Year 3 & 4* and/or *Year 5 & 6 lists* spelt correctly?
Have you checked to make sure that you have remembered your spelling rules when changing a word to a ***plural***, or adding a ***suffix*** etc.?
Have you used a ***dictionary*** to check the spelling of *ambitious, historical, technical, topical, scientific* or *challenging vocabulary?*
Have you used a ***thesaurus*** to check the meaning of a word before substituting it?

A CHECKLIST WHEN WRITING FOR THE PURPOSE OF DISCUSSING WITH OTHERS

These types of tests include... Balanced arguments, Essays, Newspaper articles, Opinion pieces, Reviews etc.

Text Features:
First, check to see if your writing needs and has the following text features for what you've been writing.

General features required of discussion texts:
Does your ***introduction*** engage the reader and state what you are writing about?

Have you used ***paragraphs*** for your *middle sections* with *topic sentences*, *to structure arguments* and/or *share a balanced view?*

Does your ***end paragraph*** round your piece off and create a sense of completion? e.g. *a summary paragraph, firming stating your opinion, confirming your view etc.*

Next, check your grammar and the sentences you've written...
Have you used a range of ***different fronted adverbials, openers*** and ***sentence starters*** across your writing? e.g. *for your introduction, conclusion* etc.

Have you effectively used ***subordinating conjunctions*** in various positions in your writing?

Have you used a range of ***adverbials*** to create *cohesion* across and within your sentences?

Have you included ***noun phrases/expanded noun phrases*** to describe in greater detail?

Are there ***modal verbs*** used to convey degrees of probability?

Have you used the ***subjunctive form*** – *made suggestions* to the *reader* - for *formal* structure?

Have you used ***relative clauses*** to provide additional and supporting detail?

Have you varied your sentence lengths for purpose? e.g. *long sentences to enhance information; short sentences for impact and effect etc.*

Have you used **synonym**s to help avoid repetition?

Have you maintained a *formal/impersonal tone* as appropriate?

Have you attempted to use the **passive voice** to maintain an *impersonal tone*?

Are there a range of different **conjunction**s used to join **clauses**?

Have you tried to remain as **unbiased** as possible when presenting your **balanced argument**?

Have you justified your **opinion**, providing **evidence** to support it?

Have you **read aloud** your sentences to check they make complete sense to the reader?

Is your writing **cohesive**? Does it *flow*?

Now check for all the punctuation you could have used...

Are **capital letters** used at the *start of* - and **full stops** used at the *end of* - each sentence?

Have you used **capital letters** for **proper nouns/the pronoun I?**

Have you used **paragraph**s to group related points and/or ideas?

Have you included **headings/subheadings** when required?

Are there **commas** after **fronted adverbials**, for **parenthesis**, for lists and for **subordinate clauses**?

Have you also used **commas** - along with **brackets** or **dashes** - for *emphasis,* **parenthesis** or *incidentals*?

Have you also used **brackets** or **dashes** to explain *historical, technical, topical or scientific vocabulary*?

Have you used **apostrophes** for contraction?

Have you also used **apostrophes** to show possession, including for **plural nouns**?

Have you used **exclamation marks** appropriately?

Are there also **question marks** in speech and for **rhetorical**

166

questions?
Have *speech marks* been used correctly and are accurately punctuated before and within the ***inverted commas***?
Have you attempted to use other higher-level ***punctuation*** for effect? e.g. ***ellipsis, hyphens*** etc.
Have you used ***semi-colons*** to either join related ***clauses*** or when needed and appropriate?
Have you also used ***semi-colons*** to punctuate complex lists, including when using ***bullet points*** and to structure ***repetition***?
Have you used ***colons*** correctly? e.g. to add further detail in a new ***clause***, to introduce *lists* or *sections* etc.
Have you also used ***colons*** and ***semi-colons*** to list *features, attractions* or *arguments* when needed?

Time to check your handwriting carefully...
Is your *handwriting **joined*** and ***legible***?
Have you checked to make sure that you have not joined any of your ***capital letters*** to the rest of your writing?
Are all of your letters the correct *shape* and *size*?
Have you written your ***ascenders*** and ***descenders*** correctly?

Finally, make sure that you check all of your spellings...
Have you checked you have spelt all common ***homophones*** correctly?
Are all the ***high frequency words*** you have learned or used from the *Year 3 & 4* and/or *Year 5 & 6 lists* spelt correctly?
Have you checked to make sure that you have remembered your spelling rules when changing a word to a ***plural***, or adding a ***suffix*** etc.?
Have you used a ***dictionary*** to check the spelling of any *ambitious, technical, historical, scientific* or *challenging vocabulary included*?
Have you used a ***thesaurus*** to check the meaning of a word before substituting it?

YOUNG WRITERS' CHECKLIST FOR THE END OF KEY STAGE 2

Finally, depending on your age and year group, check your writing against these checklists based upon what the Department for Education says you'll need to have to make sure you're exactly where you need to be to be an 'expected writer' by the end of Year 6...

To write towards the expected standard for Key Stage 2, by the end of Year 4 you must make sure that:

All your sentences start with a **capital letter**.

Your statements and all other sentences end with **full stops**.

Your question sentences end with a **question mark**.

Your exclamations end with **exclamation marks** (including *How* and *What* sentences).

Paragraphs are used to organise your main ideas.

Commas are used in a list (including *adjectival lists*).

You have used appropriate descriptive words (*adjectives, synonyms, adverbs*) etc. in your stories to help describe settings and characters.

You have used appropriate features (*structural devices*) in non-narrative writing to help it be clear to the reader, e.g. *headings, sub-headings, bullet points*.

You have written for a *specific reason*, and the *purpose* of your writing is obvious.

Your written text begins and ends appropriately, showing *cohesion* and flow.

All of your **contracted words** written contain an **apostrophe** to show **omission - letters removed**. e.g. *don't = do not / you're = you are / it's = it is.*

Your **spelling** is accurate and correct, especially for words in the *Year 3* and *4* spelling lists. (Words from the *Year 5 and 6* spellings lists have been attempted and are mostly correct).

Your *handwriting* is both **joined** and **legible** (it is clear and easy to read).

To write at the expected standard for Key Stage 2 by the end of Year 6 you must also make sure that:

You are aware of your target readers and have selected the appropriate language for that audience *(e.g. **first person** in a diary & direct address in persuasion).*

You have appropriately described the atmosphere in your narratives *(e.g. You have used adventurous **synonyms** and **antonyms** of more common words to create a more detailed atmosphere).*

Any dialogue you have written uses ***inverted commas/speech marks*** to mark the exact words spoken and helps explain/convey a character and move the action along in narratives.

You have chosen the appropriate *vocabulary* and *grammar* to express the level of ***formality*** needed to meet the requirements of the piece you are writing *(e.g. **contractions** in dialogue, **passive verbs** in arguments, **modal verbs** for degrees of possibility in articles etc..).*

You have used **adverbials** in sentences to explain *how, where* or *when* something has happened *(these are adverbs made up of more than one word).* This also helps give clarity to other related sentences and assists with joining ideas within and across **paragraphs**, *also known as* **cohesion**.

You have used some **coordinating conjunctions** (***and, but, or*** etc.) and simple **subordinating conjunctions** (*if, that, when, because* etc.) to join **main clauses** in some sentences to create **cohesion**.

You have used adventurous **synonyms** of more common words to build *cohesion* across your writing.

The *tense* of your writing is clear and consistent with correct **verbs** chosen (the **verbs** agree to help create clear *past, present* and *future tenses).*

You have used **pronouns** to refer to previously mentioned things.

You have used **commas** between **adjectives** to show pauses and to make the meaning of each sentence clear to the reader.

You have used a variety of **punctuation** including **colons, semi-colons, dashes, hyphens** and **ellipses** mostly correctly.

Your spelling is mostly correct for words in the *Year 5 and 6 spelling lists*, and you are able to use a dictionary to check the correct spelling of any *adventurous* or *ambitious words* used.

All of the **proper nouns** you have written are **capitalised**.

Your handwriting is always *joined* and easily *readable*.

You can write at *speed* and maintain regular *spacing, letter size, formation* and *writing consistency* when doing so.

Your writing has a clear *purpose*, and it is suitable for the intended audience it is written for (e.g. *your instructions are clear and can be easily followed*).

You are able to use a range of different **conjunctions**, sometimes in different parts of the sentence (*the beginning, middle* or *end*). e.g. *in addition, alternatively, consequently, meanwhile, as a result, similarly, nevertheless, on the other hand etc.*

To write with a greater depth than that of an expected writer for Key Stage 2, by the end of Year 6 you must also make sure that:

You have marked **apostrophes** to show both *possession* and *omission*.

You can appropriately demonstrate controlled shifts in levels of *formality* - by choosing precise vocabulary and changing sentence structures — using either **standard** or **non-standard English,** depending upon the purpose of the piece you're writing.

You are able to demonstrate that you have drawn from the **examples/models** of writing you have studied or the books you've read to make your writing more effective, ensuring that:
- *it has the appropriate features and form required*
- *it communicates a clear purpose*
- *it speaks well to its target audience*
- *it makes sense as a complete joined-up piece of writing*
- *it consistently stays on topic throughout*

You consistently write sentences of different lengths and ensure that they start in a variety of ways (*with **verbs, adverbials, prepositions** etc.*) often being **multi-clause sentences** too.

You are also able to include *one-, two- and three-word sentences – using **imperative verbs*** – for added dramatic effect.

You are able to make your writing multi-sensory by referring to your senses - *touch, taste, sight sound* and *smell* - and you can confidently express clear *emotion*s through *behaviour* or *action*.

You have also made clear the different language features of *speech* and writing:

- in speech: your words may be **contracted** more often than usual
- it may be more or less **formal** depending upon the purpose
- some *well-chosen and adapted* grammar differences you've used will be evident
- speech written may also include *colloquial* or *slang* words or expressions that are less likely in writing

You will have effectively included **colons** and **semi-colons** to mark the boundaries between **independent clauses**.

You are able to use **KS2 punctuation** correctly - including **ellipses** of expected words - to make your meaning obvious, avoiding any confusion, as well as helping to make your communication **clear** and **coherent** to the reader.

AUTHOR'S NOTE

I hope *A Handbook for Young Writers* helps you with your writing, especially when at school.

However, please remember one final thing – writers write first and worry about whether they've got everything they need in their writing after they've read through and edited their work.

You see, Jonas Lane's only rule for writing is to just write for the love and enjoyment of it, writing freely without any fear of failure.

That's the most important writing rule you'll ever need to know......

INDEX

A
ADJECTIVES · *10*
ADVERBIALS · *15*
ADVERBS - COMPARATIVE AND SUPERLATIVE · *17*
ADVERBS ENDING -LY · *11*
ADVERBS NOT ENDING -LY · *14*
ALLITERATION · *19*
ANTONYMS · *20*
APOSTROPHES FOR CONTRACTION · *21*
APOSTROPHES FOR POSSESSION · *21*
APOSTROPHES FOR PLURAL POSSESSION · *22*

C
CHARACTER / PERSONALITY TRAITS · *31*
CHARACTER / SETTING NAMES · *25*
CHARACTER DESCRIPTION · *23*
CHECKLIST FOR DISCUSSING WITH OTHERS · *165*
CHECKLIST FOR ENTERTAINING OTHERS · *151*
CHECKLIST FOR INFORMING OTHERS · *156*
CHECKLIST FOR PERSUADING OTHERS · *161*
COLONS · *32*
COMPARATIVE CONJUCTIONS · *34*
CONJUNCTIONS · *33*
CONTRASTIVE CONJUCTIONS · *35*
COORDINATING CONJUNCTIONS · *33*

D
DASHES · *36*
DETERMINERS · *36*

E
EMOTIVE LANGUAGE · *38*
END OF KEY STAGE 2 YOUNG WRITERS' CHECKLIST · *168*
EXCELLENT ENDINGS · *40*
EXPANDED NOUN PHRASES · *69*

F
FRONTED ADVERBIALS · *43*

H
HOMOPHONES AND NEAR-HOMOPHONES · *45*
HYPERBOLES AND EXAGGERATION · *49*
HYPHENS · *50*

I
IDIOMS · *51*
IMPERATIVE - BOSSY - VERBS · *53*
IRREGULAR PLURALS · *88*

J
JUXTAPOSITIONS · *54*

M
METAPHORS · *55*
MNEMONICS · *57*
MODAL VERBS · *58*

N
NOUN PHRASES · *69*
NOUNS - ABSTRACT NOUNS · *67*
NOUNS – COLLECTIVE NOUNS · *59*
NOUNS – COMMON NOUNS · *59*
NOUNS – PROPER NOUNS / CAPITALISATION · *61*

O
ONOMATOPOEIA · *70*
OXYMORONS · *71*

P
PARAGRAPHING · *72*
PARENTHESIS · *75*
PATHETIC FALLACY · *76*
PERSONIFICATION · *76*
PERSUASIVE LANGUAGE · *77*
PLURALS · *86*
PLURALS – NOUNS THAT DON'T CHANGE · *89*
PREFIXES · *81*
PREPOSITIONAL PHRASES · *80*
PREPOSITIONS · *78*

R
RELATIVE PRONOUNS · *90*
RHETORICAL QUESTIONS · *91*
RULE OF THREE / POWER OF THREE · *92*

S
SAID ALTERNATIVES · *93*
SEMI-COLONS · *98*
SENTENCE OPENERS – INTRODUCTIONS · *105*
SENTENCE OPENERS – ADDITIONAL INFORMATION · *104*
SENTENCE OPENERS – COMPARISONS · *104*

SENTENCE OPENERS – CONCLUSIONS · *106*
SENTENCE OPENERS – ORDER · *103*
SENTENCE OPENERS - PLACE · *103*
SENTENCE OPENERS - TIME · *102*
SETTING DESCRIPTIONS · *99*
SHOW NOT TELL · *96*
SIMILES · *101*
SPELLINGS – NATIONAL CURRICULUM WORDS KEY STGE 2 · *148*
SPELLINGS – THE FIRST 300 HIGH FREQUENCY WORDS · *146*
SPELLINGS AND SPELLING RULES · *137*
SUBORDINATING CONJUNCTIONS · *33*
SUFFIXES – GENERAL LIST AND MEANING · *122*
SUFFIXES – GENERAL RULES · *116*
SUPER STORY STARTS · *107*
SYNONYMS · *125*

V

VERB ALTERNATIVES · *131*
VERBS · *128*

Also by Jonas Lane
Slipp In Time
Grammarticus
The Last of the Unicorns
Slipp, Sliding Away
Poppy Copperthwaite: Spellcaster
Locked Down
Another Time, Slipp!
Dragon Chasers: The Knight School
Nona's Ark
Suped and Duped
There's Many a Slipp!
Wilde and Dangerous Things
Poetic Licence
Poppy Copperthwaite: Spelldemic
Sherwood Holmes: The Great Cake Robbery

All book titles available to purchase from
www.JonasLaneAuthor.com
or by ordering from **amazon.co.uk**

Thanks to all those that have left such wonderful comments. Authors and writers live or die by the reviews given by their readers.
Please take a moment to share your opinions and leave a review by visiting the site that you purchased this book from.

Alternatively, visit Jonas at his website as he would welcome your feedback.

Printed in Great Britain
by Amazon

44062654R00099